U0901439

故宫博物院藏

# 中国古代窑址标本　浙江（下）

# THE SPECIMENS OF ANCIENT CHINESE KILNS IN THE COLLECTION OF THE PALACE MUSEUM

ZHEJIANG VOLUME　III

故宫博物院编　冯小琦 / 主编

COMPILED BY THE PALACE MUSEUM
THE CHIEF COMPILER: FENG XIAOQI

故　宫　出　版　社
THE FORBIDDEN CITY PUBLISHING HOUSE

# 东阳窑

窑址在浙江省东阳市，1963年发现九处窑址，20世纪70年代后期又续有发现。东阳窑始烧于唐而终于北宋，因其唐属婺州，可视其为唐婺州窑的一部分。故宫博物院部分专家学者20世纪80年代、2009年调查了东阳葛府、歌山窑址。

葛府窑。位于市南20公里的南马镇。窑址范围在大约10里内，有三条龙窑，长约50米左右。遗物多，质量很好，大多数器物与越窑器物相似，有的壶造型、装饰与慈溪窑产品很相似。器类有碗、盘、壶、盒等，足部处理规整。碗有高矮数式，有的外壁有凹线，呈花式、花口；有的外壁有细线刻花划花。多满釉支烧，足内有垫圈烧造的痕迹。釉色有青翠、青绿、青黄多种。窑具有匣钵、喇叭形支具以及各式垫具。垫圈数量尤其多，有大小、高矮多种；匣钵多为M形，有大小之分，小的在其他瓷窑中少见，有的匣钵底略平。

歌山窑。在市北，窑址在村边，离公路不远。器类有碗、杯、瓶等。青黄、青绿色釉，光泽较差。烧法与葛府窑相似，但胎釉较葛府窑器物粗糙。有少量饰划花篦划或篦点纹，似金华窑产品。垫圈支烧。

# Dongyang Kiln

Dongyang kiln is located in Dongyang City, Zhejiang Province. Nine kiln sites were found in 1963 and more were found in late 1970s. It started to fire in Tang dynasty and ended in Northern Song dynasty. Since Dongyang belonged to Wuzhou in Tang dynasty, Dongyang kiln can be regarded as a part of Wuzhou kiln. Experts from the Palace Museum investigated kiln sites at Gefu and Geshan in the 1980s and in 2009.

Gefu is in Nanma Town, 20 kilometers south of Dongyang City. The kiln site lasts about 5 kilometers. Within the range, there are three dragon kiln sites of about 50 meters in length. Many relics of good quality in nature were found at the site and most of which are similar to that of Yue kiln. Some pots are very close to that of Cixi kiln in term of shaping and decoration. Porcelains found are bowls, plates, pots, boxes, etc., all with well-treated bottom. There are several types of bowls, for instance, high or short, flower-shaped or with flower rim resulted from the concave lines appeared on the outer wall. Some bowls are with incised design outside. Bowls were usually glazed fully and fired with supporters. Thus, inside the bottom, traces of supporters can be found. Glaze is in bright green, bluish green, greenish yellow, etc. Many varieties of kiln furniture had been found at the sites.

Geshan is in the northern part of the city. It is by a village and not far from a road. Porcelains found are bowls, cups, vases, etc. Glaze is in greenish yellow or bluish green and poor in luminosity. Its firing technique is similar to that of Gefu, but quality of glaze and body is interior to the later. A small number of Geshan wares are with incised design of comb patterns or dots, which are very close to Jinhua kiln products. Geshan wares were fired with supporting rings.

**东阳（葛府）窑遗址保护碑**
Monument for protecting the ruin of Dongyang kiln at Gefu

**东阳（葛府）窑遗址窑具遗存**
Pileup of kiln furniture parts at the ruin of Dongyang kiln at Gefu

1074　**五代至宋　青釉刻花莲瓣纹高足温碗标本**

From Five Dynasties to Song dynasty

Specimen of green glaze warming bowl with high stem and incised lotus-petal design

1075 **宋 青釉花口瓶标本**
Song dynasty
Specimen of green glaze vase with flower rim

1076 **宋 青釉罐标本**
Song dynasty
Specimen of green glaze jar

1077 **宋　青釉壶标本**

Song dynasty

Specimens of green glaze pot

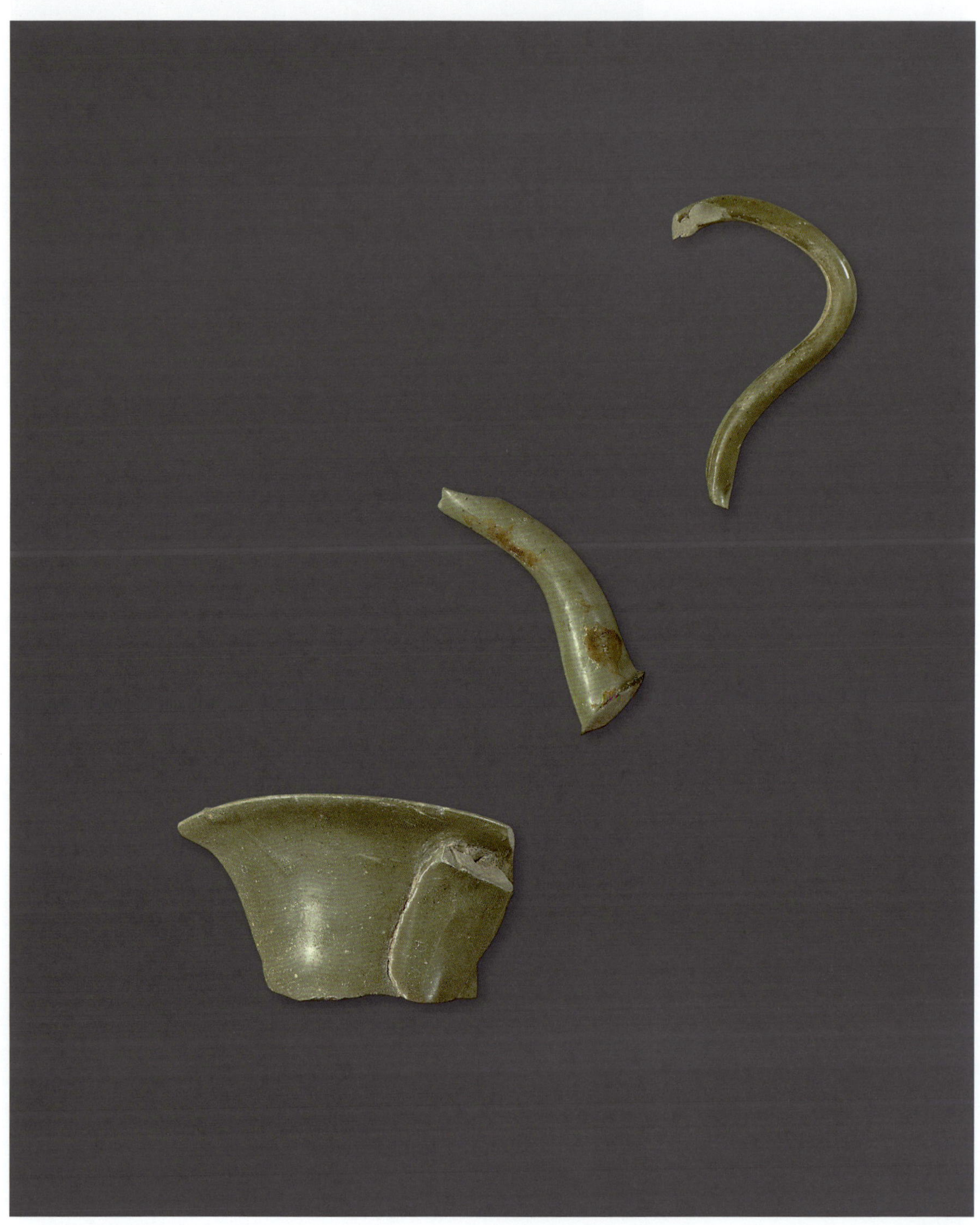

1078 **宋 青釉瓜棱壶标本**

Song dynasty

Specimens of green glaze melon-shaped pot

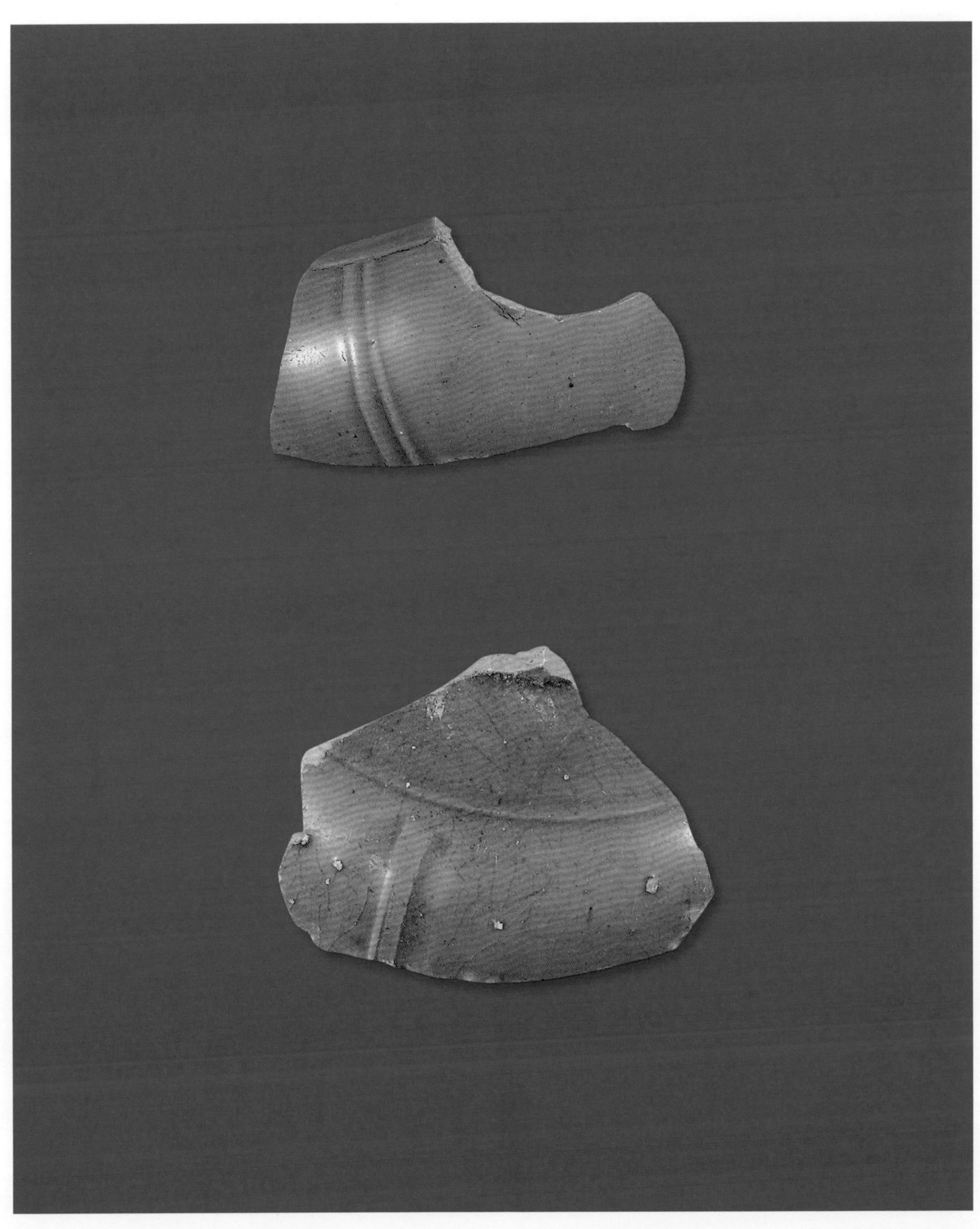

1079 **宋 青釉花式碗标本**

Song dynasty

Specimens of green glaze flower-shaped bowl

1080　**宋　青釉花式碗标本**

Song dynasty

Specimens of green glaze flower-shaped bowl

1081 **宋 青釉花式碗标本**
Song dynasty
Specimen of green glaze flower-shaped bowl

1082 **宋 青釉盘标本**
Song dynasty
Specimen of green glaze plate

1083 **宋 青釉盘标本**

Song dynasty

Specimens of green glaze plate

1084 **宋 青釉盘标本**
Song dynasty
Specimens of green glaze plate

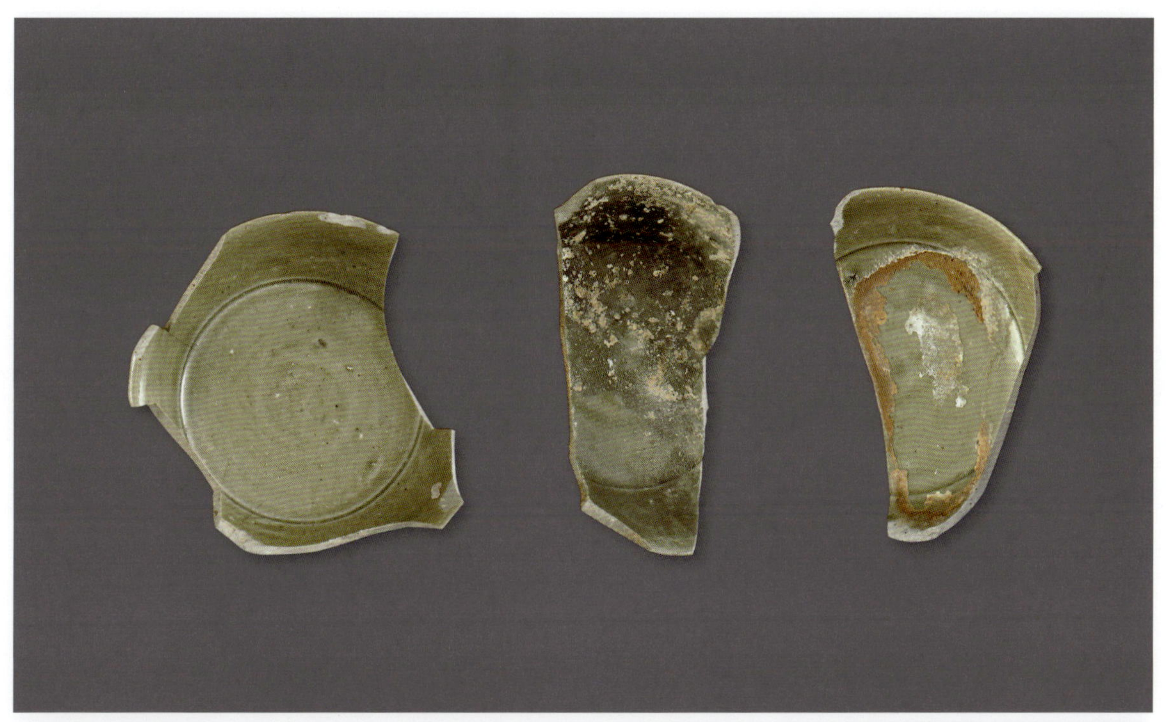

1085　宋　青釉刻花花卉纹供器标本
Song dynasty
Specimen of green glaze sacrifice ware with incised flower design

1086　宋
青釉刻划花花卉纹带系罐标本
Song dynasty
Specimen of green glaze jar with handles and incised flower design

1087 **宋 窑具标本**
Song dynasty
Specimens of kiln furniture

**东阳（歌山）窑遗址保护碑**
Monument for protecting the ruin of Dongyang kiln at Geshan

**东阳（歌山）窑遗址瓷片遗存**
Pileup of porcelain parts at the ruin of Dongyang kiln at Geshan

1088　**宋　青釉带系罐标本**
Song dynasty
Specimen of green glaze jar with handles

1089　**宋　青釉碗标本**
Song dynasty
Specimen of green glaze bowl

1090 **宋　青釉碗标本**
Song dynasty
Specimen of green glaze bowl

1091 **宋 青釉碗标本**
Song dynasty
Specimen of green glaze bowl

1092 **宋 青釉弦纹罐标本**
Song dynasty
Specimens of green glaze jar with string design

1093 宋 青釉划花篦划纹碗标本

Song dynasty

Specimens of green glaze bowl with comb-incised design

1094　宋　窑具标本
Song dynasty
Specimen of kiln furniture

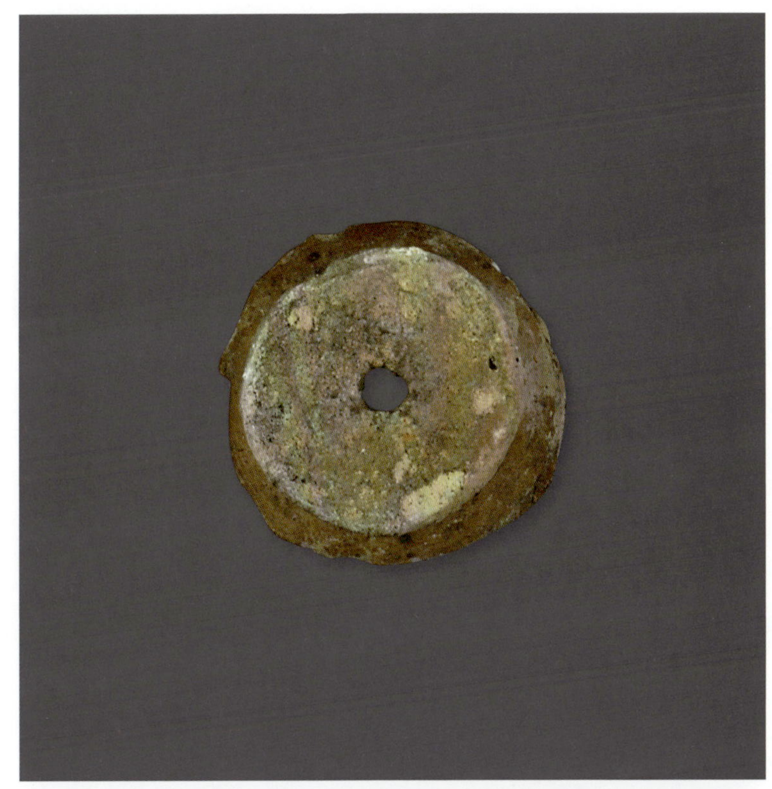

1095　宋　窑具标本
Song dynasty
Specimens of kiln furniture

1096　宋　青釉壶标本

Song dynasty

Specimens of green glaze pot

1097 **宋 青釉瓜棱壶标本**
Song dynasty
Specimen of green glaze melon-shaped pot

1098 **宋 青釉瓜棱壶标本**
Song dynasty
Specimen of green glaze melon-shaped pot

1099 **宋 青釉瓜棱壶标本**

Song dynasty

Specimens of green glaze melon-shaped pot

1100 **宋 青釉瓜棱壶标本**
Song dynasty
Specimens of green glaze melon-shaped pot

1101 **宋 青釉带系壶标本**
Song dynasty
Specimen of green glaze pot
with handles

1102　**宋　青釉枕标本**
Song dynasty
Specimen of green glaze pillow

1103　**宋　青釉碗标本**
Song dynasty
Specimen of green glaze bowl

1104 宋 青釉碗标本
Song dynasty
Specimens of green glaze bowl

1105 **宋 青釉碗标本**
Song dynasty
Specimen of green glaze bowl

1106 **宋 青釉碗标本**
Song dynasty
Specimens of green glaze bowl

1107 **宋　青釉花式碗标本**
Song dynasty
Specimen of green glaze flower-shaped bowl

1108 **宋　青釉盏托标本**
Song dynasty
Specimen of green glaze saucer

1109　宋　青釉盘标本
Song dynasty
Specimen of green glaze plate

1110　宋　青釉盘标本
Song dynasty
Specimen of green glaze plate

1111　宋　青釉花式杯标本
Song dynasty
Specimen of green glaze flower-shaped cup

1112 **宋　青釉刻花莲瓣纹碗标本**
Song dynasty
Specimens of green glaze bowl with incised lotus-petal design

1113　**宋　青釉刻花花瓣纹钵标本**
Song dynasty
Specimen of green glaze alms bowl with incised flower-petal design

1114　**宋　青釉刻花花卉纹盘标本**
Song dynasty
Specimen of green glaze plate with incised floral design

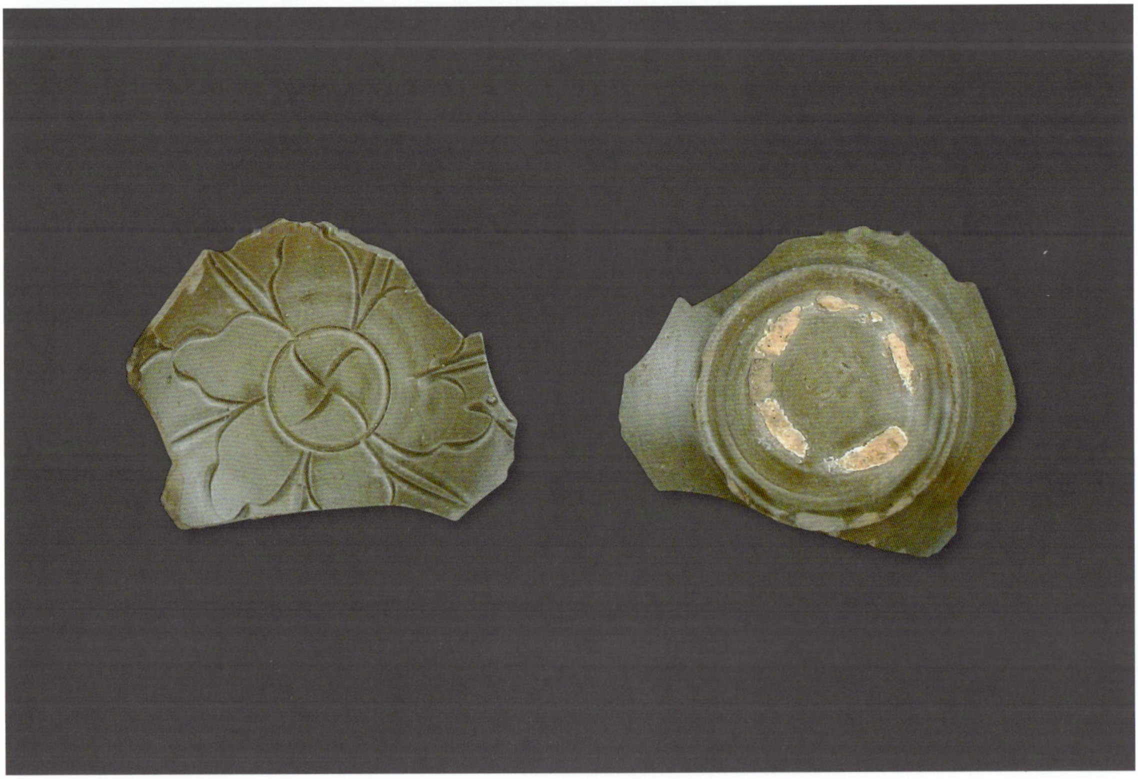

1115 **宋　青釉刻花花卉纹盘标本**

Song dynasty

Specimens of green glaze plate with incised floral design

1116　**宋　青釉刻划花花卉纹盘标本**

Song dynasty

Specimen of green glaze plate with incised floral design

1117　**宋**

**青釉刻划花花卉纹杯标本**

Song dynasty

Specimen of green glaze cup with incised floral design

1118　**宋**

**青釉刻划花莲瓣纹杯标本**

Song dynasty

Specimen of green glaze cup with incised lotus-petal design

# 龙游窑

窑址位于浙江省龙游县上圩头乡方坦村，20 世纪 80 年代及 2008 年故宫博物院部分专家学者考察了此窑。

龙游窑为唐代瓷窑。所烧器物以罐为主，装饰有划花水波纹；双系罐的系部印有较深的印纹装饰。主要烧制乳浊釉、青釉器物，兼烧少量褐釉器物。有些青釉因烧结程度不高，釉面剥落较为严重。

# Longyou Kiln

Longyou kiln is located at Fangtan Village, Shangxutou Town, Longyou County, Zhejiang Province. Experts from the Palace Museum visited the kiln in the 1980s and in 2008.

Longyou kiln is a Tang dynasty porcelain kiln. Produce of the kiln are mainly jars with incised wave design. Jars with two handles are with stamped design pressed deeper on their handles. The main output of the kiln is opaque glaze, green glaze and a small number of brown glaze artifacts. Because kiln temperature is not high enough, the glaze layer of some of the wares flakes off the body very seriously.

1119 **唐　青釉双系罐标本**

Tang dynasty

Specimens of green glaze jar with two handles

1120 **唐　青釉划花水波纹罐标本**

Tang dynasty

Specimens of green glaze jar with incised wave design

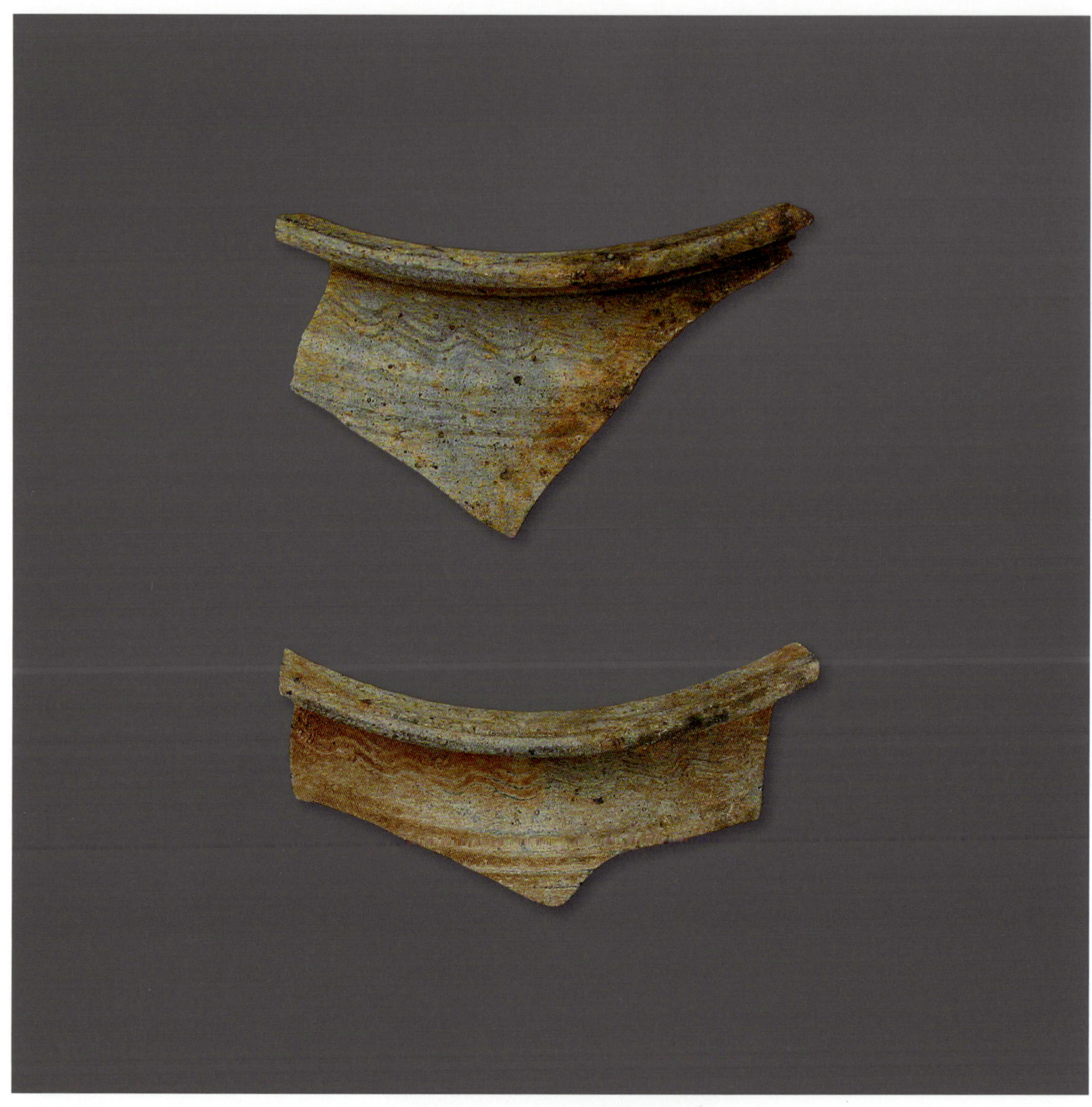

1121 **唐 乳浊釉罐标本**

Tang dynasty

Specimen of opaque glaze jar

# 衢州窑

窑址在浙江省衢州县。故宫博物院部分专家学者 20 世纪 80 年代调查了衢州冬瓜潭、沈家山两处窑址，2008 年又调查了冬瓜潭、沈家山、梁公塘窑址。

衢州窑为唐宋时期瓷窑。唐代窑址在衢州河东乡上叶村发现三处，主要烧制乳光釉、月白釉、天青釉几个品种，造型有壶、罐等，施釉仅及口下的碗和盏等。宋代窑址有冬瓜潭窑，烧青釉、青釉褐彩、青酱釉、黑酱釉、黑釉等品种。青釉敞口圈足碗内划线纹，采用叠烧工艺，碗里有支烧痕。划花盘采用满釉支烧，属越窑类型，釉色深青。执壶为扁柄，有的壶身为六瓣形，有一种壶高达 50~60 厘米。罐、壶质地较粗。青釉褐彩器标本有折沿盆、壶、瓶、罐，釉较薄，为灰青色，饰酱褐彩，是该窑最具代表性的品种。青酱釉器物有盒、盏、六瓣花口小杯，越窑型浮雕莲瓣纹碗等。黑酱釉器物有碗、壶等，造型与青釉相同。黑釉器物有刻菊瓣纹碗，刻线较粗，施釉不到底，一种是用半圆形工具剔去地子；一种是先刻单线，再刻成菊瓣纹。

从总体看衢州窑的青釉釉色较深，是金华地区青瓷的特点。

# Quzhou Kiln

Quzhou kiln is located in Quzhou County, Zhejiang Province. Experts from the Palace Museum investigated kiln sites at Dongguatan and Shenjiashan in the 1980s and in 2008. They investigated kiln site at Lianggongtang in 2008.

Quzhou kiln is a porcelain kiln of Tang and Song dynasty. The three kiln sites found at Shangye Village of Hedong Town are from Tang dynasty. There fired opalescent, moon-white and sky blue glaze wares, such as pots, jars and partially glazed bowls and saucers and so on. Dongguatan kiln site is from Song dynasty, where green glaze, green glaze with decoration of brown color, greenish dark reddish brown glaze, blackish dark reddish brown glaze, black glaze, etc. were fired. Green glaze bowls with flat mouth, ring foot and incised design of double lines inside were put into the kiln and fired one inside the other. In the center of such bowls spur marks were left behind. Green glaze plates with incised design were fired with supports, thus, they are fully glazed and similar to that of Yue kiln. The glaze color is in dark green. Ewers have flat handles. Some ewers are six-flower-petal-shaped. There is a pot whose height is up to 50-60 cm. The texture of jars and pots is relatively coarse. Specimens of green glaze wares with decoration of brown color collected are basins with everted flange, pots, vases and jars. The glaze of such kind of wares is relatively thin and in grayish green. It is the kind of ware that best represents the kiln. Greenish dark reddish brown glaze wares are boxes, saucers, small cups with rim in shape of six flower petals, Yue kiln alike bowls with design of lotus-petals in relief, etc. Blackish dark reddish brown glaze wares are bowls, pots, etc. Their shaping is similar to that of green glaze. Black glaze wares are bowls with incised design of chrysanthemum. They are partially glazed and lines incised are broader. Generally speaking, the glaze of Quzhou kiln ware is relative darker and it is the feature of green glaze in Jinhua region.

衢州（冬瓜潭）窑遗址
Ruin of Quzhou kiln at Dongguatan

1122 **宋　青釉罐标本**
Song dynasty
Specimen of green glaze jar

1123 **宋　青釉双系罐标本**
Song dynasty
Specimens of green glaze jar with two handles

1124　**宋　青釉壶标本**

Song dynasty

Specimens of green glaze pot

1125 **宋　青釉碗标本**

Song dynasty

Specimens of green glaze bowl

1126 **宋　青釉碗标本**
Song dynasty
Specimen of green glaze bowl

1127 **宋　青釉刻线纹碗标本**
Song dynasty
Specimen of green glaze bowl with incised design of lines

1128 **宋　青釉刻划花纹碗标本**
Song dynasty
Specimen of green glaze bowl with incised design

1129 **宋　青釉里刻划花外刻线纹碗标本**
Song dynasty
Specimen of green glaze bowl with incised design inside and incised lines outside

1130 **宋　青釉里刻划花外刻线纹碗标本**

Song dynasty

Specimens of green glaze bowl with incised design inside and incised lines outside

1131 **宋 青釉划花篦划纹碗标本**

Song dynasty

Specimen of green glaze bowl with comb-incised design

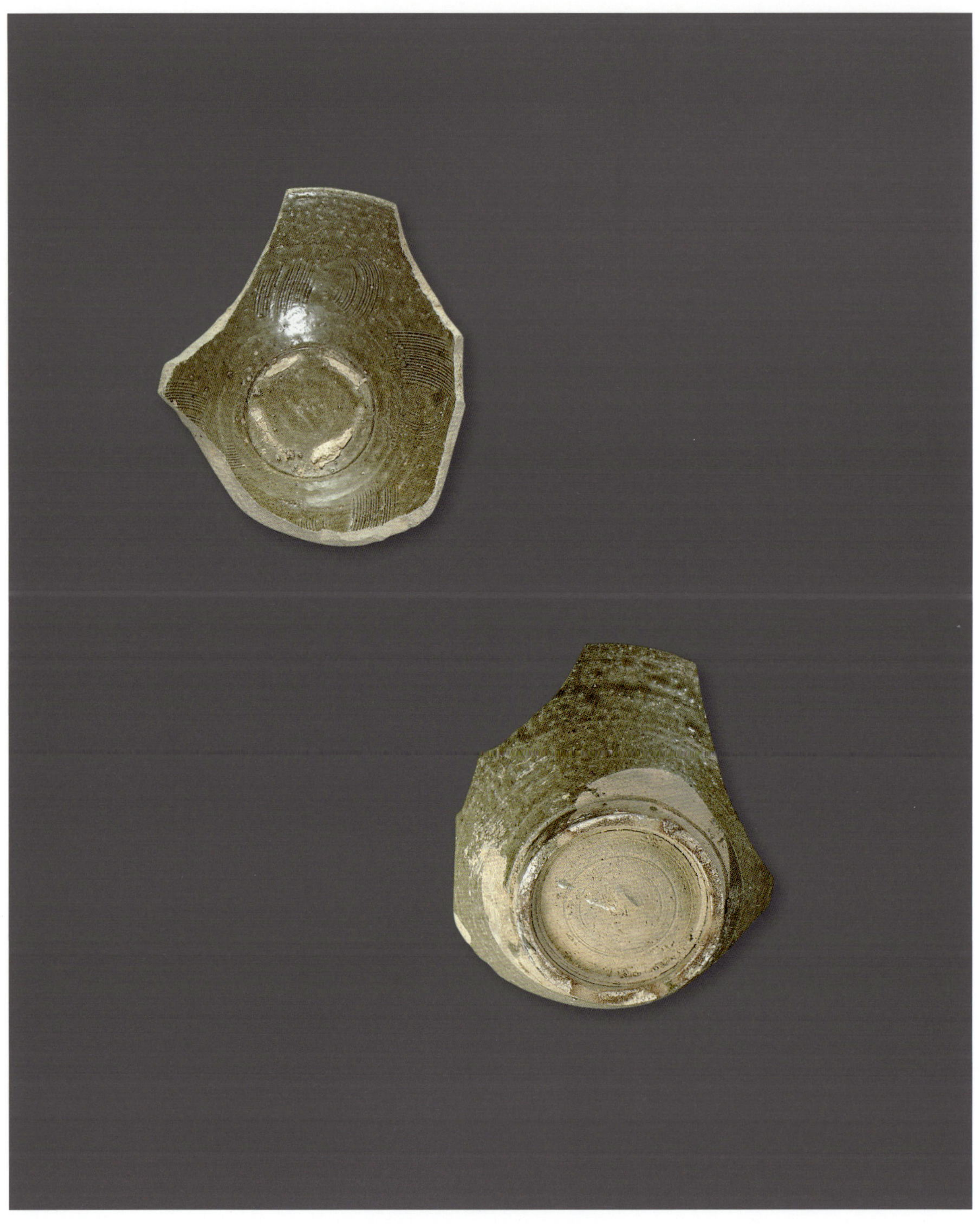

1132 **宋 青釉划花篦划纹碗标本**

Song dynasty

Specimens of green glaze bowl with comb-incised design

1133 **宋 青釉划花篦划纹碗标本**

Song dynasty

Specimen of green glaze bowl with comb-incised design

1134 **宋**

**青釉里划花篦划纹外刻线纹碗标本**

Song dynasty

Specimen of green glaze bowl with comb-incised design inside and incised lines outside

1135 **宋 青釉褐彩花卉纹罐标本**

Song dynasty

Specimens of green glaze jar with floral design in brown color

1136 **宋　青釉褐彩花卉纹双系罐标本**

Song dynasty

Specimens of green glaze jar with two handles and floral design in brown color

1137　**宋　青釉褐彩花卉纹壶（罐）标本**

Song dynasty

Specimens of green glaze pot (jar) with floral design in brown color

1138　**宋　青釉褐彩花卉纹壶（罐）标本**

Song dynasty

Specimens of green glaze pot (jar) with floral design in brown color

1139　宋　青釉褐彩花卉纹缸标本

Song dynasty

Specimens of green glaze vat with floral design in brown color

1140　**宋　青釉褐彩花卉纹盆标本**

Song dynasty

Specimens of green glaze basin with floral design in brown color

1141　**宋　青釉褐彩花卉纹盆标本**
Song dynasty
Specimen of green glaze basin with floral design in brown color

1142　**宋　青釉褐彩鱼纹盆标本**
Song dynasty
Specimen of green glaze basin with fish design in brown color

1143　**宋**
**青釉褐彩花卉纹折沿盆标本**
Song dynasty
Specimen of green glaze basin with everted flange and floral design in brown color

1144　宋　青釉褐彩花卉纹折沿盆标本

Song dynasty

Specimens of green glaze basin with everted flange and floral design in brown color

1145 **宋　青白釉罐标本**
Song dynasty
Specimen of bluish white glaze jar

1146 **宋　青白釉碗标本**
Song dynasty
Specimen of bluish white glaze bowl

1147　**宋　青白釉碗标本**
Song dynasty
Specimen of bluish white glaze bowl

1148　**宋　青白釉刻线纹碗标本**
Song dynasty
Specimen of bluish white glaze
bowl with incised design of lines

1149 **宋 黑釉碗标本**
Song dynasty
Specimen of black glaze bowl

1150 **宋 黑褐釉罐标本**
Song dynasty
Specimens of black brown glaze jar

1151　宋　黑褐釉碗标本
Song dynasty
Specimen of black brown glaze bowl

1152　宋　黑褐釉碟标本
Song dynasty
Specimen of black brown glaze saucer

1153 宋 褐釉带系罐标本
Song dynasty
Specimen of brown glaze jar with handles

1154 宋 褐釉双复系罐标本
Song dynasty
Specimen of brown glaze jar with handles

1155 宋 褐釉壶标本
Song dynasty
Specimens of brown glaze pot

1156 **宋　褐釉壶标本**

Song dynasty

Specimens of brown glaze pot

1157　**宋　褐釉壶标本**

Song dynasty

Specimen of brown glaze pot

1158 **宋　褐釉壶标本**

Song dynasty

Specimens of brown glaze pot

1159　**宋　褐釉双系壶标本**
Song dynasty
Specimen of brown glaze pot with two handles

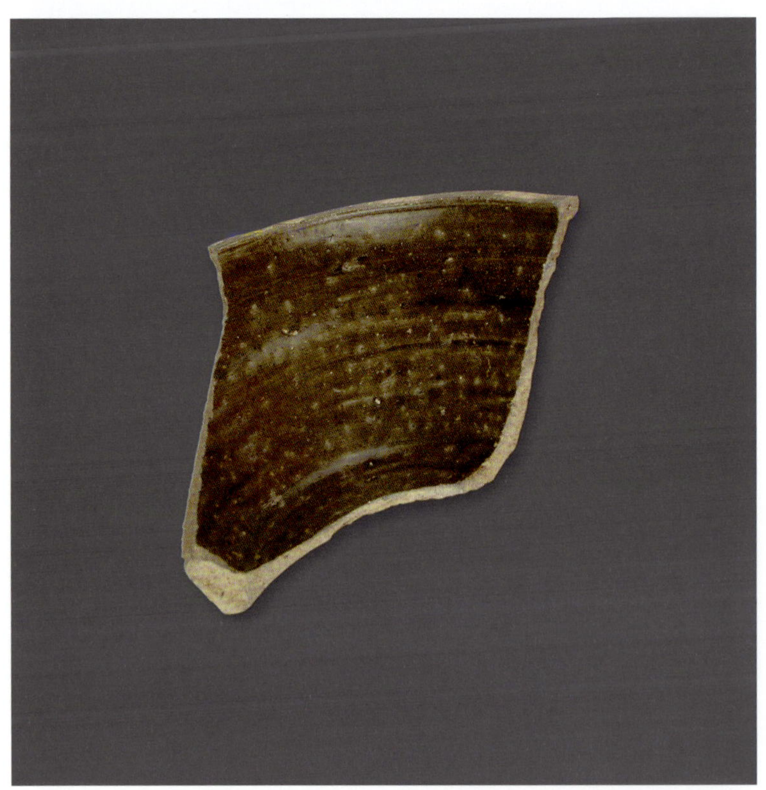

1160　**宋　褐釉盆标本**
Song dynasty
Specimen of brown glaze basin

1161 **宋 窑具标本**
Song dynasty
Specimen of kiln furniture

1162 **宋 窑具标本**
Song dynasty
Specimen of kiln furniture

**衢州（沈家山）窑遗址瓷片遗存**

Pileup of porcelain parts at the ruin of Quzhou kiln at Shenjiashan

1163 **宋 青釉瓜棱壶标本**

Song dynasty

Specimen of green glaze melon-shaped pot

1164 **宋 青釉瓜棱壶及窑具标本**

Song dynasty

Specimen of green glaze melon-shaped pot and kiln furniture

1165 **宋　青釉碗标本**

Song dynasty

Specimens of green glaze bowl

1166 **宋 青釉碗标本**

Song dynasty

Specimens of green glaze bowl

1167 **宋　黑褐釉碗标本**

Song dynasty

Specimens of black brown glaze bowl

1168　**宋　黑褐釉杯标本**
Song dynasty
Specimen of black brown glaze cup

1169　**宋　酱黄釉花式碗标本**
Song dynasty
Specimen of dark brownish yellow glaze flower-shaped bowl

**衢州（梁公塘）窑遗址保护碑**
Monument for protecting the ruin of Quzhou kiln at Lianggongtang

1170 **宋　青釉褐彩花卉纹罐标本**

Song dynasty

Specimens of green glaze jar with floral design in brown color

1171 **宋**

**青釉褐彩花卉纹器盖标本**

Song dynasty

Specimens of green glaze cover with floral design in brown color

1172　**宋　青釉褐彩花卉纹缸标本**

Song dynasty

Specimens of green glaze vat with floral design in brown color

1173 **宋　青釉褐彩花卉纹折沿盆标本**

Song dynasty

Specimen of green glaze basin with everted flange and floral design in brown color

1174　**宋　青釉褐彩花卉纹折沿盆标本**

Song dynasty

Specimens of green glaze basin with everted flange and floral design in brown color

1175 **宋 褐釉瓶标本**

Song dynasty

Specimens of brown glaze vase

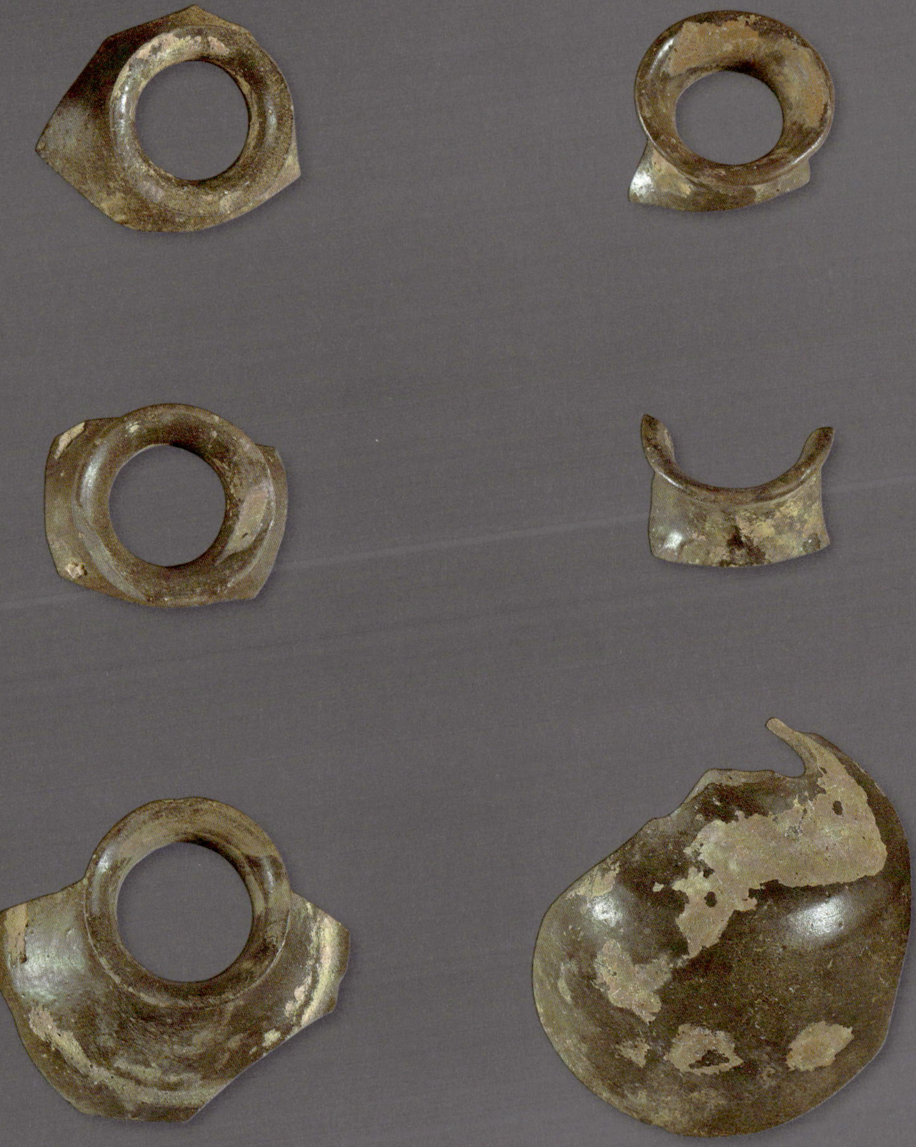

1176 **宋　褐釉壶标本**
Song dynasty
Specimen of brown glaze pot

1177 **宋　褐釉弦纹带系罐标本**
Song dynasty
Specimen of brown glaze jar with
design of strings and handles

# 江山窑

窑址在浙江省江山县，主要分布在江山县源口、桐子坞、前坞、大坝两侧和达河。故宫博物院部分专家学者 20 世纪 80 年代调查了桐子坞、前坞、大坝两侧窑址，2008 年调查了达河窑址群。

江山窑为宋至明代瓷窑。宋代烧青白瓷、青瓷及黑瓷，以青白瓷为多。由于距江西较近，器物造型和纹饰受景德镇及南丰窑影响，有不少相似之处。江山窑出土青白瓷中有印纹方瓶，底印阳文“周家功夫”四字，“功夫”是宋代工艺品中常见用语。青釉里篦划纹外刻线纹碗，在福建同安、松溪及浙江龙泉宋元窑址中都有发现，浙西地区尚属首次发现。黑釉碗的口施青釉，似模仿北方地区黑釉白口碗的装饰，由于受原料制约，只能烧出青口，这种施釉方法在南方一些瓷窑也可见到。

# Jiangshan Kiln

Jiangshan kiln is located in Jiangshan County, Zhejiang Province. Kiln sites are mainly found at Yuankou, Tongziwu, Qianwu, Dabaliangce and Dahe in Jiangshan County. Experts from the Palace Museum investigated kiln sites at Tongziwu, Qianwu and Dabaliangce in the 1980s and Dahe in 2008.

Jiangshan kiln operated from Song to Ming dynasty. In Song dynasty, the kiln fired bluish white, green and black glaze wares, with bluish white the largest in numbers. Since it is close to Jiangxi Province, shaping and decoration are affected by Jingdezhen and Nanfeng kiln. There are many similarities between them. Bluish white glaze square vase with stamped design and Chinese characters, Zhou Jia Gong Fu, stamped on its bottom was unearthed from Jiangshan kiln. Gong Fu is a common phrase in crafts of Song dynasty. Green glaze bowls with comb incised patterns inside and incised lines outside have been found at kiln sites of Song and Yuan dynasty in Tong'an and Songxi County, Fujian Province and Longquan City, Zhejiang Province. It is the first time in western Zhejiang Province to find such bowls. Black glaze bowl with green rim is an imitation of black glaze bowl with white rim in the North. Limited by raw materials in the South, Jiangshan kiln was unable to produce black glaze bowl with white rim but only green rim. This kind of glaze-applying method can be seen in some other kilns in the South.

1178 **宋 黑釉青口碗标本**

Song dynasty

Specimens of black glaze bowl with green rim

1179　**宋　黑釉青口碗标本**
Song dynasty
Specimen of black glaze bowl with green rim

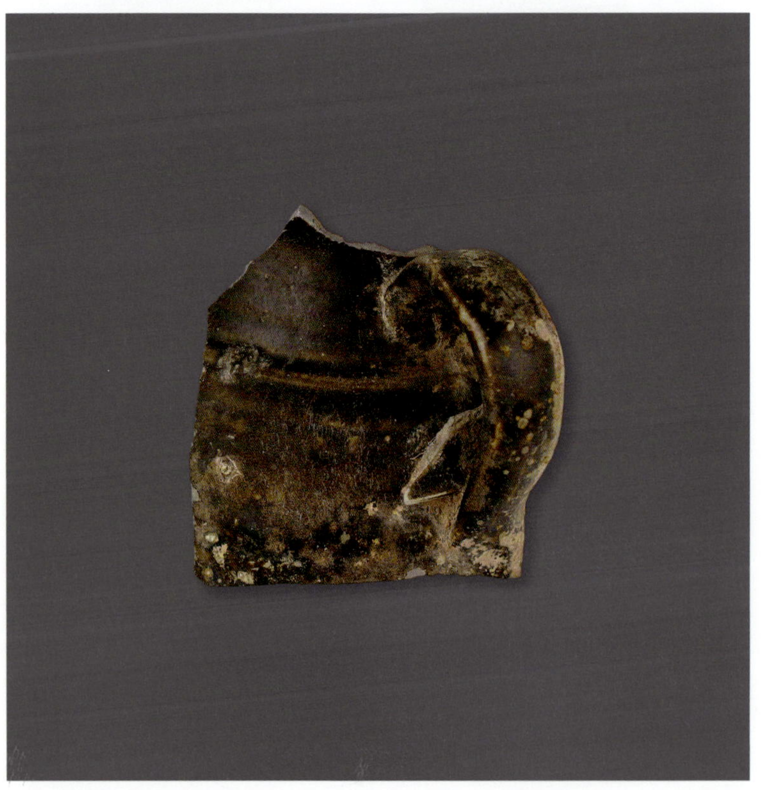

1180　**宋　黑褐釉双系罐标本**
Song dynasty
Specimen of black brown glaze jar with two handles

1181　南宋至元　青白釉花口瓶标本
From Southern Song dynasty to Yuan dynasty
Specimens of bluish white glaze vase with flower rim

1182　**南宋至元　青白釉壶标本**
From Southern Song dynasty to Yuan dynasty
Specimen of bluish white glaze pot

1183　**南宋至元　青白釉瓜棱壶标本**
From Southern Song dynasty to Yuan dynasty
Specimens of bluish white glaze melon-shaped pot

1184　**南宋至元**

**青白釉瓜棱壶标本**

From Southern Song dynasty to Yuan dynasty

Specimen of bluish white glaze melon-shaped pot

1185　**南宋至元**

**青白釉三足炉标本**

From Southern Song dynasty to Yuan dynasty

Specimen of bluish white glaze burner with three-legged design

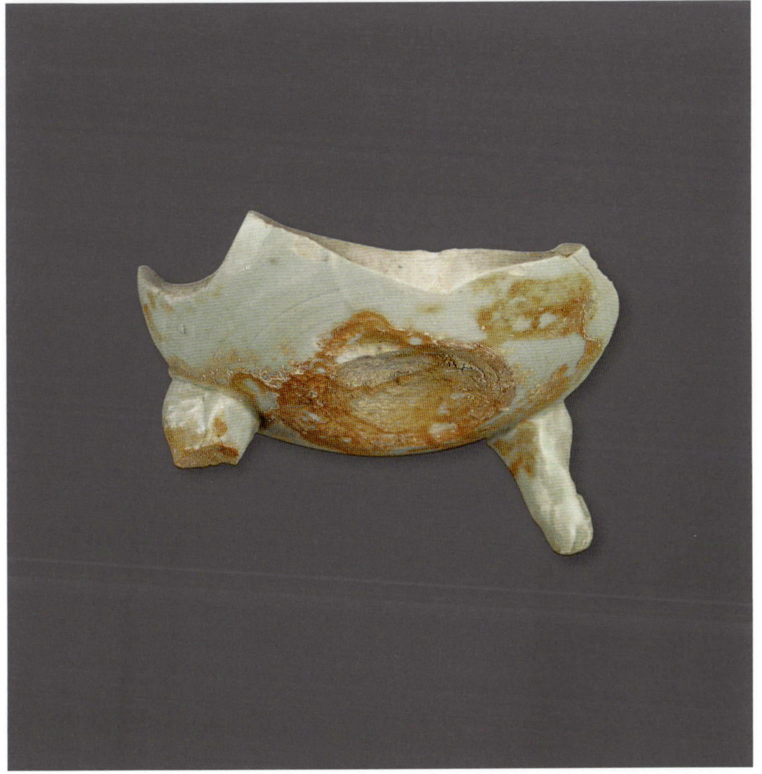

1186　**南宋至元　青白釉菊瓣式盒标本**

From Southern Song dynasty to Yuan dynasty

Specimens of bluish white glaze chrysanthemum-shaped box

1187 **南宋至元　青白釉器盖标本**
From Southern Song dynasty to
Yuan dynasty
Specimen of bluish white glaze cover

1188 **南宋至元　青白釉碗标本**
From Southern Song dynasty to
Yuan dynasty
Specimen of bluish white glaze bowl

1189 南宋至元 青白釉印花花卉纹瓶标本
From Southern Song dynasty to Yuan dynasty
Specimens of bluish white glaze vase with stamped floral design

1190　**南宋至元　青白釉印花花卉纹瓶标本**
From Southern Song dynasty to Yuan dynasty
Specimens of bluish white glaze vase with stamped floral design

1191　**南宋至元　青白釉印花花卉纹瓶标本**
From Southern Song dynasty to Yuan dynasty
Specimens of bluish white glaze vase with stamped floral design

1192　**南宋至元　青白釉印花花卉纹瓶标本**
From Southern Song dynasty to Yuan dynasty
Specimen of bluish white glaze vase with stamped floral design

1193　**南宋至元　青白釉印花卷枝纹罐标本**
From Southern Song dynasty to Yuan dynasty
Specimen of bluish white glaze jar with stamped design of branch scrolls

1194　**南宋至元　青白釉印花花卉纹罐盖标本**
From Southern Song dynasty to Yuan dynasty
Specimen of bluish white glaze jar cover with stamped floral design

1195　南宋至元　青白釉印花八卦纹炉标本
From Southern Song dynasty to Yuan dynasty
Specimens of bluish white glaze burner with stamped design of eight divinatory trigrams

1196 **南宋至元 青白釉印花八卦纹三足炉标本**

From Southern Song dynasty to Yuan dynasty

Specimens of bluish white glaze burner with stamped design of eight divinatory trigrams and with three legs

1197　**南宋至元　青白釉印花花卉纹菊瓣式盒标本**
From Southern Song dynasty to Yuan dynasty
Specimens of bluish white glaze chrysanthemum-petal-shaped box with stamped floral design

1198　**南宋至元　青白釉印花花卉纹菊瓣式盒标本**
From Southern Song dynasty to Yuan dynasty
Specimens of bluish white glaze chrysanthemum-petal-shaped box with stamped floral design

1199 **南宋至元　青白釉印花花卉纹高足杯标本**

From Southern Song dynasty to Yuan dynasty

Specimens of bluish white glaze cup with high stem and stamped floral design

1200　**元至明　青白釉褐彩花卉纹碗标本**
From Yuan dynasty to Ming dynasty
Specimens of bluish white glaze bowl with design of flowers in brown

**江山（达河）窑遗址保护碑**
Monument for protecting the ruin of Jiangshan kiln at Dahe

**江山（达河）窑遗址瓷片遗存**
Pileup of porcelain parts at the ruin of Jiangshan kiln at Dahe

1201 **宋　青釉罐标本**
Song dynasty
Specimen of green glaze jar

1202 **宋　青釉碗标本**
Song dynasty
Specimen of green glaze bowl

1203 **宋　青釉碗标本**
Song dynasty
Specimen of green glaze bowl

1204 **宋　青釉凸线纹碗标本**
Song dynasty
Specimen of green glaze bowl with design of lines in relief

1205　**宋　青釉刻线纹碗标本**
Song dynasty
Specimen of green glaze bowl with incised design of lines

1206　**宋**
**青釉刻划花篦划纹碗标本**
Song dynasty
Specimens of green glaze bowl with comb-incised design

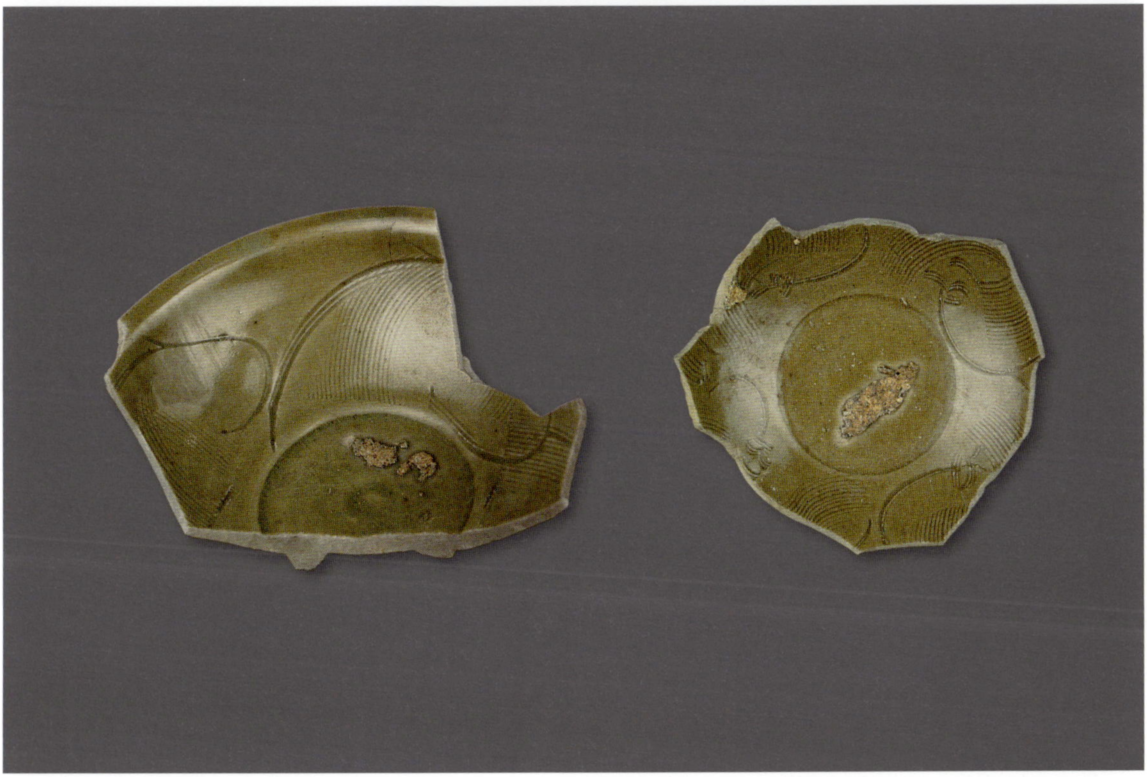

1207 **宋　青釉里刻划花篦划纹外刻线纹碗标本**

Song dynasty

Specimen of green glaze bowl with comb-incised design inside and incised lines outside

1208 **宋　黑釉碗标本**
Song dynasty
Specimen of black glaze bowl

1209 **宋　黑釉盏托标本**
Song dynasty
Specimen of black glaze saucer

1210 **宋　黑釉青口碗标本**
Song dynasty
Specimen of black glaze bowl with green rim

1211 **宋 青釉缸标本**

Song dynasty

Specimens of green glaze vat

1212 **宋 青釉缸标本**
Song dynasty
Specimen of green glaze vat

1213 **宋 青釉碗标本**
Song dynasty
Specimens of green glaze bowl

1214　**宋　青釉碗标本**

Song dynasty

Specimens of green glaze bowl

1215 **宋 青釉碗标本**

Song dynasty

Specimens of green glaze bowl

1216 **宋 青釉里划花篦划纹外刻线纹碗标本**

Song dynasty

Specimens of green glaze bowl with comb-incised design inside and incised lines outside

1217 **宋　青釉里划花篦划纹外刻线纹碗标本**

Song dynasty

Specimens of green glaze bowl with comb-incised design inside and incised lines outside

1218　**宋　黑釉双系罐标本**

Song dynasty

Specimens of black glaze jar with two handles

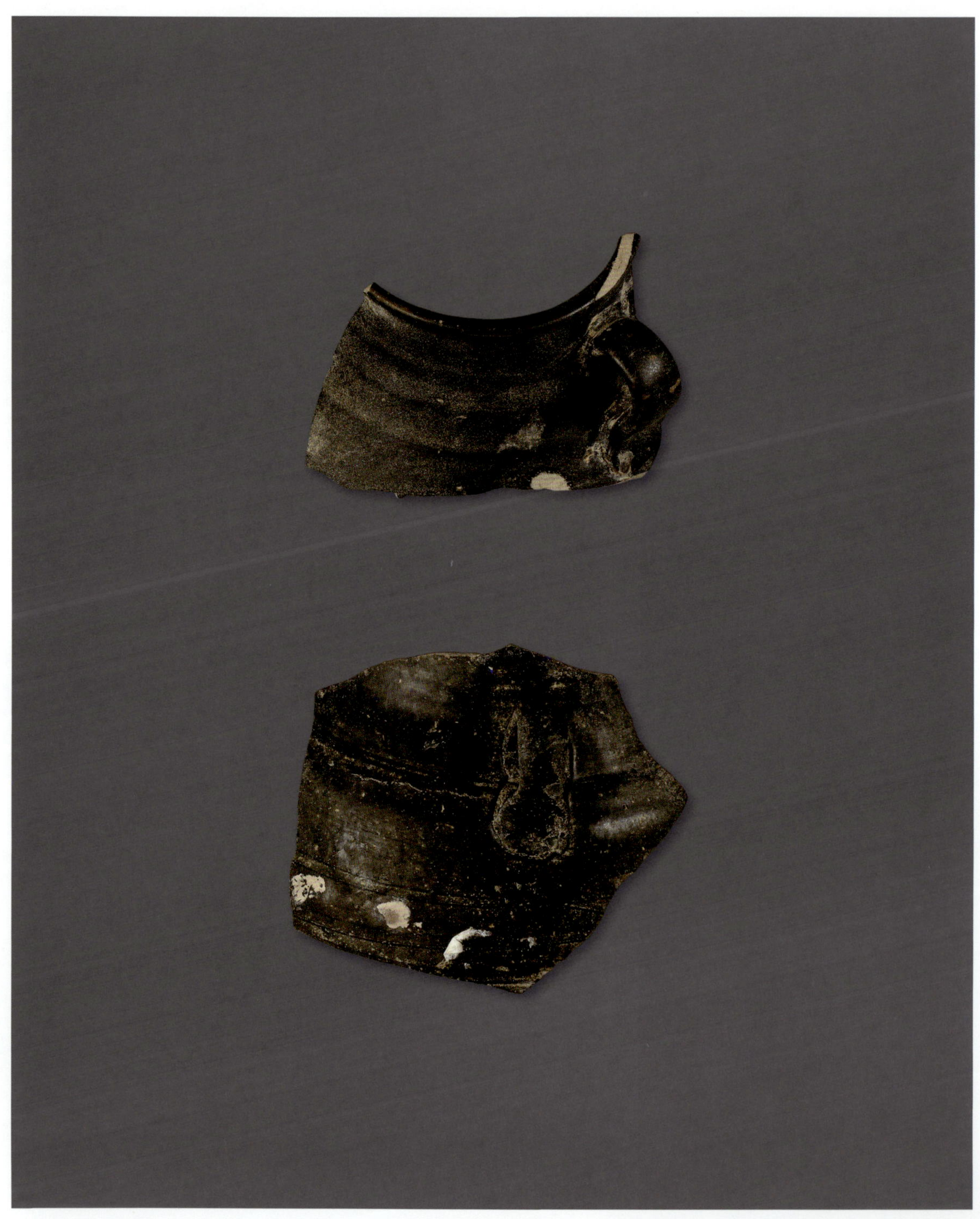

1219 **宋　黑釉碗标本**
Song dynasty
Specimens of black glaze bowl

1220 **宋 黑釉青口碗标本**

Song dynasty

Specimens of black glaze bowl with green rim

1221 **宋　黑釉青口碗标本**

Song dynasty

Specimens of black glaze bowl with green rim

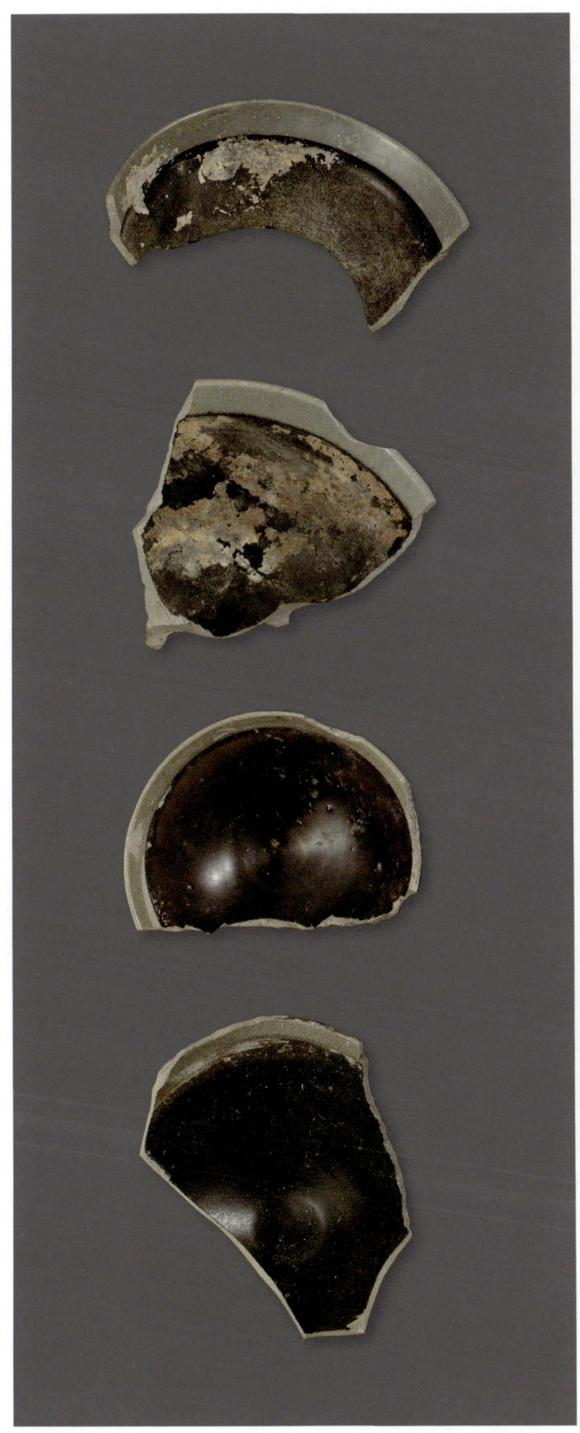

1222　**宋　黑酱釉碗标本**

Song dynasty

Specimen of dark brownish black glaze bowl

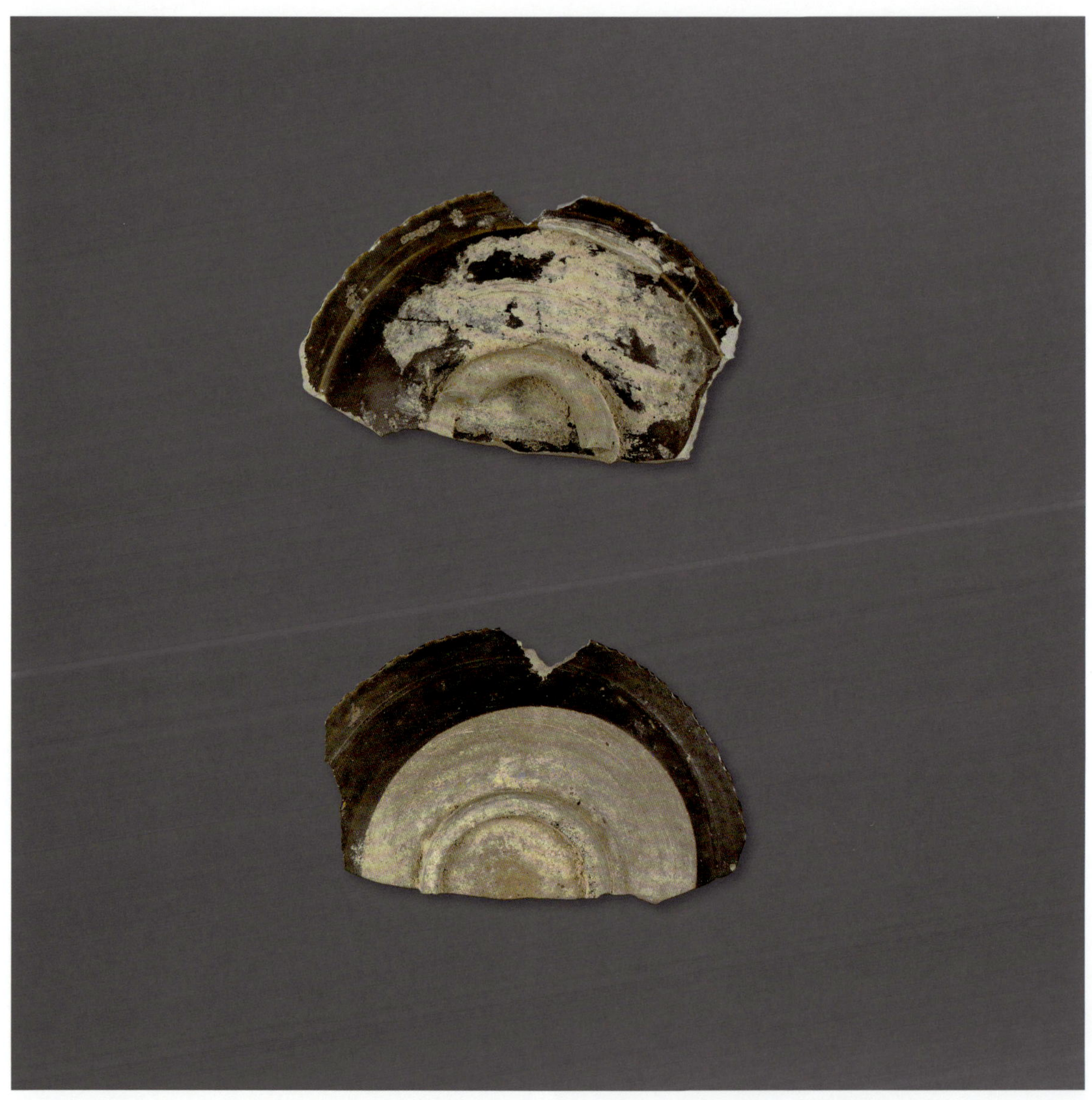

1223　**南宋至元　青白釉瓶标本**
From Southern Song dynasty to
Yuan dynasty
Specimen of bluish white glaze vase

1224　**南宋至元**
**青白釉花口瓶标本**
From Southern Song dynasty to
Yuan dynasty
Specimen of bluish white glaze
vase with flower rim

1225 **南宋至元**
**青白釉瓜棱壶标本**
From Southern Song dynasty to Yuan dynasty
Specimen of bluish white glaze melon-shaped pot

1226 **南宋至元 青白釉炉标本**
From Southern Song dynasty to Yuan dynasty
Specimen of bluish white glaze burner

1227　南宋至元　青白釉三足炉标本
From Southern Song dynasty to Yuan dynasty
Specimens of bluish white glaze burner with three legs

1228 **南宋至元　青白釉菊瓣式盒标本**

From Southern Song dynasty to Yuan dynasty

Specimens of bluish white glaze chrysanthemum-petal-shaped box

1229　**南宋至元　青白釉碗标本**

From Southern Song dynasty to Yuan dynasty

Specimens of bluish white glaze bowl

1230　**南宋至元　青白釉高足杯标本**
From Southern Song dynasty to Yuan dynasty
Specimen of bluish white glaze cup with high stem

1231　**南宋至元　青白釉印花带系瓶标本**
From Southern Song dynasty to Yuan dynasty
Specimen of bluish white glaze vase with handles and stamped design

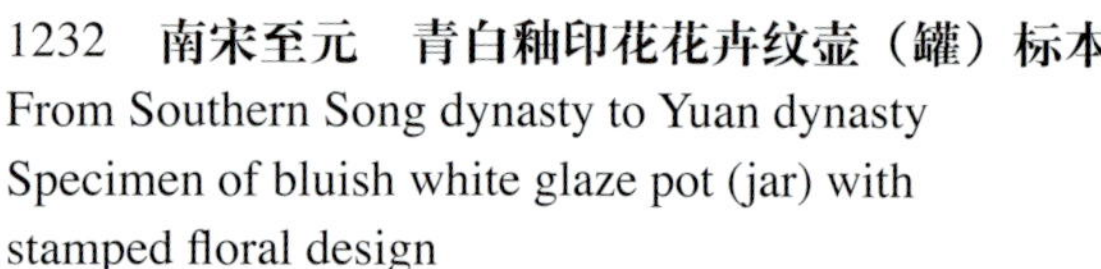

1232　**南宋至元　青白釉印花花卉纹壶（罐）标本**
From Southern Song dynasty to Yuan dynasty
Specimen of bluish white glaze pot (jar) with stamped floral design

1233　**南宋至元　青白釉印花花卉纹壶（罐）标本**

From Southern Song dynasty to Yuan dynasty

Specimens of bluish white glaze pot (jar) with stamped floral design

1234 **南宋至元　青白釉印花壶标本**
From Southern Song dynasty to Yuan dynasty
Specimens of bluish white glaze pot with stamped design

1235 **南宋至元　青白釉印花八卦纹炉标本**
From Southern Song dynasty to Yuan dynasty
Specimens of bluish white glaze burner with stamped design of eight divinatory trigrams

1236 **南宋至元　青白釉印花八卦纹炉标本**
From Southern Song dynasty to Yuan dynasty
Specimen of bluish white glaze burner with stamped design of eight divinatory trigrams

1237 **南宋至元　青白釉印花花卉纹菊瓣式盒标本**
From Southern Song dynasty to Yuan dynasty
Specimen of bluish white glaze chrysanthemum-petal-shaped box with stamped floral design

1238 **南宋至元　青白釉印花盖标本**
From Southern Song dynasty to Yuan dynasty
Specimen of bluish white glaze cover with stamped design

1239 **宋　窑具标本**

Song dynasty

Specimens of kiln furniture

1240 **宋　窑具标本**
Song dynasty
Specimens of kiln furniture

1241 **宋　窑具标本**
Song dynasty
Specimens of kiln furniture

**江山（达河三卿口）窑遗址**
Ruin of Jiangshan kiln at Dahesanqingkou

1242　元　**青釉炉标本**

Yuan dynasty

Specimen of green glaze burner

1243　**元　青釉碗标本**

Yuan dynasty

Specimens of green glaze bowl

1244 **元　青釉盘标本**

Yuan dynasty

Specimens of green glaze plate

1245 元 青釉弦纹罐标本

Yuan dynasty

Specimen of green glaze jar with strings

1246 元 青釉印花花卉纹碗标本

Yuan dynasty

Specimens of green glaze bowl with stamped flower design

1247 **元 窑具标本**
Yuan dynasty
Specimen of kiln furniture

1248 **元 窑具标本**
Yuan dynasty
Specimens of kiln furniture

# 遂昌窑

该窑为元明时期窑址群。2009 年故宫博物院部分专家学者考察了遂昌窑 Y1、Y2 两处窑址。

Y1 堆积比较丰富，主要器物为元代风格。常见厚胎碗，外刻突起的莲瓣纹，有的里心刻朵花纹。釉色有似龙泉窑风格的，也有似越窑特点的。器物足部修坯较规矩，足底心垫饼支烧。造型有碗、盘等，盘有折沿的。总体质量比较好。有的釉色很漂亮，似粉青；有的釉色深绿青翠；有的釉色泛黄。胎釉致密。精者甚至与龙泉窑上品不相上下。有的碗心好像有“清”字。窑具有匣钵、垫饼、支具等。

Y2 窑具、瓷片散落在更大的范围内。时代主要为明代。胎釉较元代瓷器粗很多，工艺也粗糙，多采用器心无釉直接垫烧。里心素胎者印有图案，有马、折枝花卉、折枝梅花、银锭、小鸟、双鱼；还有印文字者，有“广”、“常”、“福”、“寿”、“和”、“利”、“清”、“满”、“象（荣）春”等。釉色有青黄、青绿。造型有碗、折沿盘等。匣钵有 M 形，垫饼有圆形、圆饼带小托者。

# Suichang Kiln

Suichang kiln sites are in groups dated back to Yuan and Ming dynasty. In 2009, experts from the Palace Museum investigated two kiln sites named YI and YII.

Kiln site YI is rich in accumulation. Wares excavated are mainly style of Yuan dynasty. Bowls with thick body and with incised design of lotus-petal in relief outside and sometime with incised flower inside center are common. The glaze color of some of the bowls is similar to Longquan kiln style and some are with the characteristics of Yue kiln wares. Bowls, plates, plates with everted flange and such with well-treated bottom, fired using pads against bottom center, are in general good quality. Some are with very beautiful glaze, equivalent to light greenish blue. Some are with bright green glaze and some in yellowish green. All are with dense glaze and body. The top grade pieces are even comparable with Longquan kiln wares. For some of the bowls, there seems a Chinese character Qing inside the center. Kiln furniture includes saggars, pads, spurs and such.

Porcelain parts of Ming dynasty mainly were scattered in a wider range at kiln site YII. Body and glaze of Ming dynasty wares are inferior to that of Yuan dynasty and so are firing techniques. They were usually with no glaze in the center and put into kiln one inside the other directly and fired. Wares with no glaze inside center are with such stamped patterns as horse, disconnected sprays of flowers, disconnected sprays of plum, silver ingot, birds, pair fish; or with stamped Chinese character(s), for instance, Guang, Chang, Fu, Shou, He, Li, Qing, Man, Xiang (Rong) Chun, etc. Glaze is in greenish yellow or bluish green. Wares excavated here are bowls, plates with everted flange and so on. There are M -shaped saggars. Pads are round. There is a kind of pad with a small pad on top of a large round base.

**遂昌窑遗址**
Ruin of Suichang kiln

**遂昌窑遗址瓷片遗存**
Pileup of porcelain parts at the ruin of Suichang kiln

1249 **元 青釉碗标本**

Yuan dynasty

Specimens of green glaze bowl

1250　元　青釉碗标本
Yuan dynasty
Specimens of green glaze bowl

1251　元　青釉碗标本
Yuan dynasty
Specimen of green glaze bowl

1252　元　**青釉碗标本**
Yuan dynasty
Specimen of green glaze bowl

1253　元　**青釉折沿盘标本**
Yuan dynasty
Specimens of green glaze plate with everted flange

1254 元 **青釉折沿盘标本**

Yuan dynasty

Specimens of green glaze plate with everted flange

1255　元　青釉模印莲瓣纹碗标本

Yuan dynasty

Specimens of green glaze bowl with stamped lotus-petal design

1256　元　**青釉模印莲瓣纹碗标本**

Yuan dynasty

Specimens of green glaze bowl with stamped lotus-petal design

1257　元　**青釉模印莲瓣纹碗标本**

Yuan dynasty

Specimens of green glaze bowl with stamped lotus-petal design

1258　**元　青釉刻花莲瓣纹碗标本**

Yuan dynasty

Specimens of green glaze bowl with incised lotus-petal design

## 1259　元　青釉刻线纹碗标本

Yuan dynasty

Specimens of green glaze bowl with incised line design

1260 **元 青釉刻线纹碗标本**
Yuan dynasty
Specimen of green glaze bowl with incised line design

1261 **元 青釉刻线纹碗标本**
Yuan dynasty
Specimen of green glaze bowl with incised line design

1262 **元 青釉划花篦划纹碗标本**
Yuan dynasty
Specimen of green glaze bowl with comb-incised design

1263　**元至明　青釉印花花卉纹碗标本**

From Yuan dynasty to Ming dynasty

Specimens of green glaze bowl with stamped flower design

1264　元至明　青釉印花花卉纹碗标本
From Yuan dynasty to Ming dynasty
Specimens of green glaze bowl with stamped flower design

1265 **元至明 青釉印花朵花纹碗标本**
From Yuan dynasty to Ming dynasty
Specimen of green glaze bowl with stamped flower design

1266 **元至明 青釉印花朵花纹碗标本**
From Yuan dynasty to Ming dynasty
Specimen of green glaze bowl with stamped flower design

1267　元至明　青釉印花葵花纹碗标本

From Yuan dynasty to Ming dynasty

Specimen of green glaze bowl with stamped sun flower design

1268　元至明　青釉印花银锭纹碗标本

From Yuan dynasty to Ming dynasty

Specimen of green glaze bowl with stamped design of silver ingot

## 1269 元至明 青釉印花银锭纹碗标本
From Yuan dynasty to Ming dynasty
Specimens of green glaze bowl with stamped design of silver ingot

1270 **元至明 青釉印花马纹碗标本**
From Yuan dynasty to Ming dynasty
Specimen of green glaze bowl with stamped horse design

1271 **元至明 青釉印花双鱼纹碗标本**
From Yuan dynasty to Ming dynasty
Specimen of green glaze bowl with stamped design of pair fish

1272 **元至明　青釉印“常”字碗标本**

From Yuan dynasty to Ming dynasty

Specimens of green glaze bowl with stamped Chinese character Chang

1273　元至明　青釉印“福”字碗标本

From Yuan dynasty to Ming dynasty

Specimens of green glaze bowl with stamped Chinese character Fu

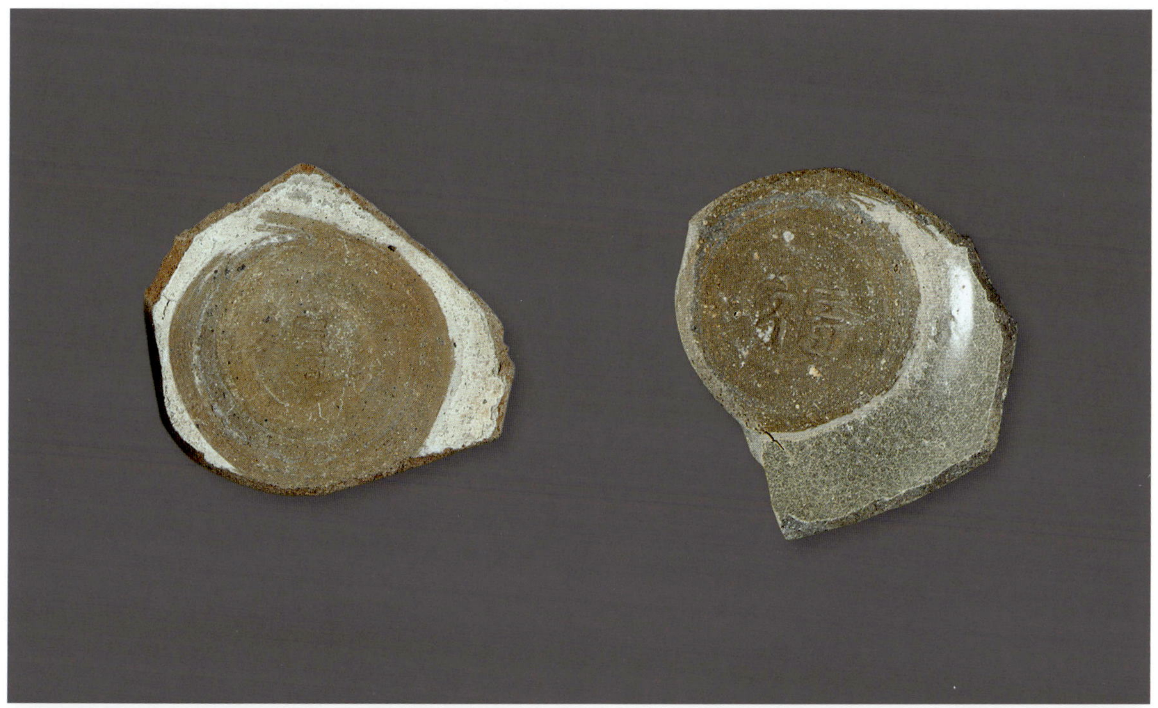

1274 元至明 青釉印“寿”字碗标本
From Yuan dynasty to Ming dynasty
Specimen of green glaze bowl with stamped Chinese character Shou

1275 元至明 青釉印“利”字碗标本
From Yuan dynasty to Ming dynasty
Specimen of green glaze bowl with stamped Chinese character Li

1276 **元至明 青釉印“春”字碗标本**
From Yuan dynasty to Ming dynasty
Specimen of green glaze bowl with stamped Chinese character Chun

1277 **元至明 青釉印“旺”字碗标本**
From Yuan dynasty to Ming dynasty
Specimen of green glaze bowl with stamped Chinese character Wang

1278 **元至明 青釉印“广”字碗标本**

From Yuan dynasty to Ming dynasty

Specimens of green glaze bowl with stamped Chinese character Guang

1279 **元至明　青釉里印“王”字外模印莲瓣纹碗标本**
From Yuan dynasty to Ming dynasty
Specimen of green glaze bowl with stamped Chinese character Wang inside and lotus-petal outside

1280 **元至明　青釉印花花卉纹盘标本**
From Yuan dynasty to Ming dynasty
Specimen of green glaze plate with stamped flower design

1281　元至明　青釉里印花朵花纹外刻莲瓣纹碗标本
From Yuan dynasty to Ming dynasty
Specimen of green glaze bowl with stamped flower design inside and incised lotus-petal outside

1282　元至明　青釉里印花莲花纹外刻线纹碗标本
From Yuan dynasty to Ming dynasty
Specimen of green glaze bowl with stamped lotus design inside and incised design of lines outside

1283 **元至明 青釉里印刻划花朵花纹外刻线纹碗标本**

From Yuan dynasty to Ming dynasty

Specimen of green glaze bowl with stamped and incised flower design inside and incised line design outside

1284　**元至明　窑具标本**
From Yuan dynasty to Ming dynasty
Specimens of kiln furniture

# 松阳窑

窑址位于松阳县城西北 20 公里的界首水井岭山，为唐宋时期瓷窑。2009 年故宫博物院部分专家学者调查了松阳窑。

在该窑一断壁上有约一尺多厚、两三米长的瓷片堆积，主要为青釉碗、罐的碎片，多数质量较粗。碗内有数个较大的支烧痕，多平底，有的有旋成璧足的线纹。小碗为小饼足，微内凹。釉色有青、青黄、浅青等。瓶、壶、罐多施半釉，底露胎。釉色粗黄者似金华窑青釉。窑址范围内匣钵很少见，只见有喇叭形支具，可能为裸烧所致。

# Songyang Kiln

Songyang kiln, a porcelain kiln dated back to Tang and Song dynasty, is located at Shuijinglingshan, Jieshou, 20 kilometers northwest of Songyang County. Experts from the Palace Museum investigated the kiln site in 2009.

A profile of the kiln shows the accumulation, mostly parts of green glaze bowls and jars of poor quality, is about 0.33 meters in height and 2-3 meters in length. Inside the bowls, there are several relatively large spur marks. Bowls are usually with flat bottom. Traces left behind on some of the bowls suggest the wall foot was made by rotating cuts. Bowls of small size have small cake-like, slightly concave foot. Glaze is in green, greenish yellow or light green. Vases, pots and jars were usually half glazed and their bottoms were unglazed. Those of poor quality glaze and in greenish yellow are similar to green glaze wares of Jinhua kiln. Few saggars can be spotted, but only supporting tools in shape of a speaker across the kiln site. The phenomenon may suggest the kiln did not use saggars when firing wares.

**松阳窑遗址**
Ruin of Songyang kiln

**松阳窑遗址瓷片遗存**
Pileup of porcelain parts at the ruin of Songyang kiln

1285 **晚唐至五代　青釉碗标本**

From Late Tang dynasty to Five Dynasties

Specimens of green glaze bowl

1286 **晚唐至五代 青釉碗标本**

From Late Tang dynasty to Five Dynasties

Specimens of green glaze bowl

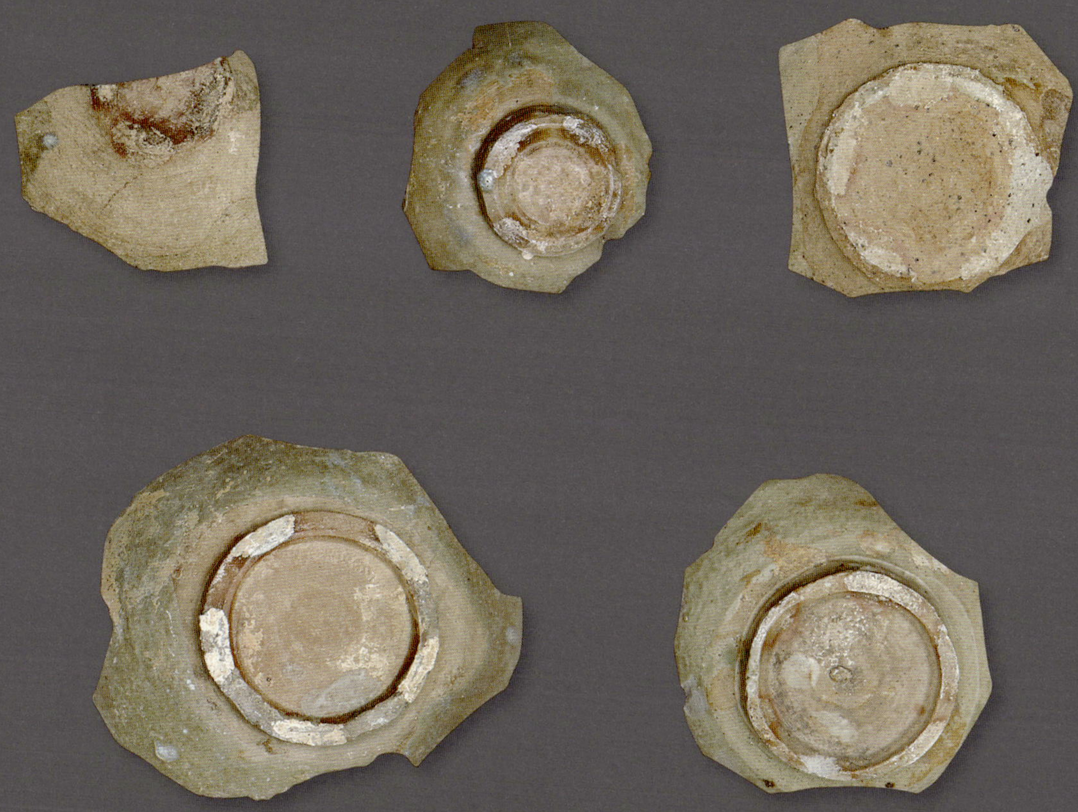

1287 **宋　青釉瓶标本**

Song dynasty

Specimens of green glaze vase

1288　**宋　青釉罐标本**
Song dynasty
Specimens of green glaze jar

1289　**宋　青釉罐标本**
Song dynasty
Specimen of green glaze jar

1290 **宋　青釉罐标本**

Song dynasty

Specimens of green glaze jar

1291 **宋　青釉带系罐标本**

Song dynasty

Specimens of green glaze jar with handles

1292 **宋 青釉带系罐标本**
Song dynasty
Specimens of green glaze jar with handles

1293 **宋 青釉双系壶标本**
Song dynasty
Specimen of green glaze pot with two handles

# 丽水窑

2007 年 12 月故宫博物院部分专家学者调查了丽水吕步坑窑与保定窑。

吕步坑窑。烧瓷历史较早。采集有青釉标本，以碗的数量为多，兼有少量钵、罐、壶、砚台等。胎质较粗，胎色较深。碗里口以下露胎，平足内凹，采用支钉支烧，支钉不很规则。窑具有垫柱、垫饼等。

保定窑。宋代烧制划花篦划纹青釉碗，釉色有青黄、青绿等；元代主要烧制龙泉窑风格的青釉碗，胎质较厚，装饰有刻划花、印花，纹饰有折枝花、菊花、莲花等。有的碗外饰弦纹，采用支钉支烧；有的碗里心露胎，直接垫烧。另还烧少量青釉罐及黑褐釉小碗，后者也采用支钉支烧。窑具有研磨器、垫圈、垫饼等。

# Lishui Kiln

Experts from the Palace Museum investigated Lishui kiln at Lübukeng and Baoding in December, 2007.

Kiln at Lübukeng started to fire earlier. Specimens collected are green glaze wares. Among them, bowls are the largest in numbers, followed by alms bowls, jars, pots, ink slabs, etc. The body of the wares is poor in quality and looks dark. Bowls are unglazed just below the rim inside and have flat, concave bottom. They were fired using irregular spurs. Kiln furniture includes supporting posts, pads, etc.

Kiln at Baoding fired green glaze wares with incised design of comb patterns in Song dynasty. Glaze is in bright green, greenish yellow, etc. It fired mainly green glaze bowls of Longquan kiln style in Yuan dynasty. With relatively thick body, decorated with incised or stamped patterns, such as disconnected sprays of flowers, chrysanthemum, lotus, strings, etc., they are fired using spurs. Some of the bowls are fired using pads instead. As a result, the inside center is without glaze. In addition, the kiln fired a few green glaze jars and small blackish brown bowls. The later was fired using spurs, too. Kiln furniture includes grinders, supporting rings, pads, etc.

**丽水（吕步坑）窑遗址保护碑**
Monument for protecting the ruin of Lishui kiln at Lübukeng

**丽水（吕步坑）窑遗址**
Ruin of Lishui kiln at Lübukeng

1294 **唐　青釉碗标本**

Tang dynasty

Specimens of green glaze bowl

1295　唐　青釉碗标本

Tang dynasty

Specimens of green glaze bowl

1296 **唐　青釉碗标本**

Tang dynasty

Specimens of green glaze bowl

1297 **唐 青釉钵标本**
Tang dynasty
Specimens of green glaze alms bowl

1298 **唐 青褐釉瓶标本**
Tang dynasty
Specimen of greenish brown glaze vase

1299 **唐　青褐釉带系罐标本**

Tang dynasty

Specimens of greenish brown glaze jar with handles

1300 **唐 青褐釉钵标本**
Tang dynasty
Specimens of greenish brown glaze alms bowl

1301 **唐 窑具标本**
Tang dynasty
Specimens of kiln furniture

**丽水（保定）窑遗址保护碑**
Monument for protecting the ruin of Lishui kiln at Baoding

**丽水（保定）窑遗址**
Ruin of Lishui kiln at Baoding

1302　**南宋至元　青釉划花篦划纹碗标本**
From Southern Song dynasty to Yuan dynasty
Specimen of green glaze bowl with comb-incised design

1303　**元　青釉碗标本**
Yuan dynasty
Specimens of green glaze bowl

1304 元 青釉碗标本
Yuan dynasty
Specimens of green glaze bowl

1305　元　青釉碗标本

Yuan dynasty

Specimen of green glaze bowl

1306　元　青釉高足杯标本

Yuan dynasty

Specimen of green glaze cup with high stem

1307　**元　青釉高足杯标本**

Yuan dynasty

Specimens of green glaze cup with high stem

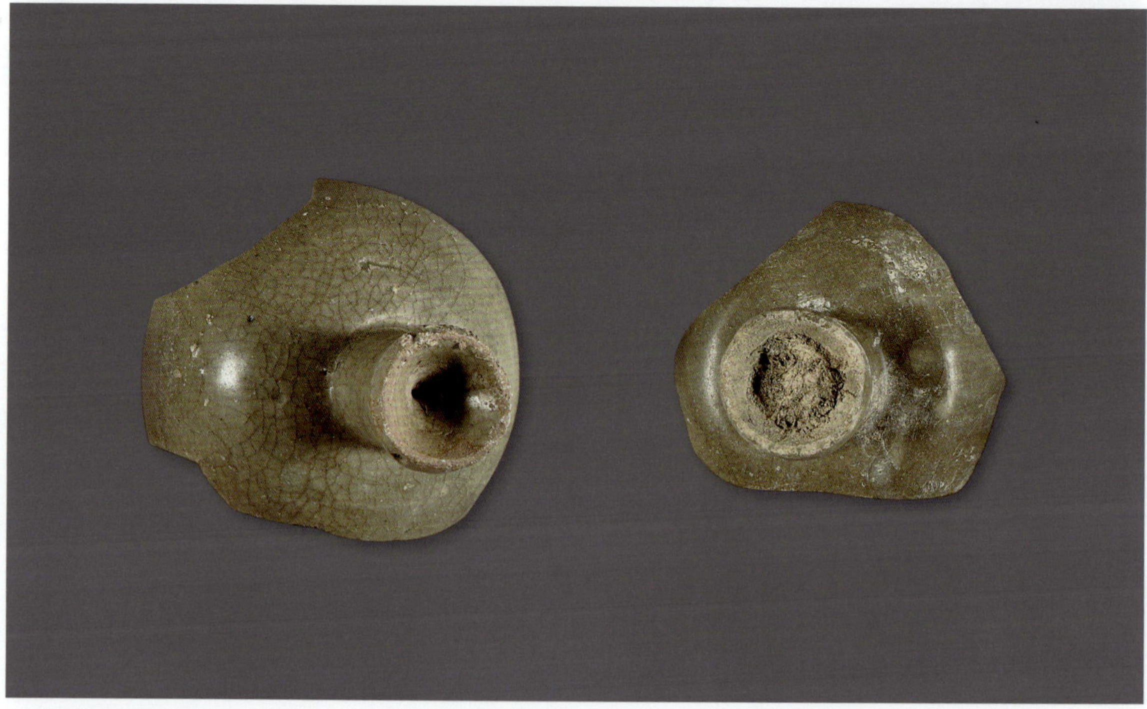

1308　**元　青釉印花莲花纹碗标本**

Yuan dynasty

Specimens of green glaze bowl with stamped lotus design

1309 元 青釉印花莲花纹碗标本

Yuan dynasty

Specimens of green glaze bowl with stamped lotus design

1310 元 青釉印花莲花纹碗标本
Yuan dynasty Specimen of green glaze bowl with stamped lotus design

1311 元 青釉印花菊花纹碗标本
Yuan dynasty Specimen of green glaze bowl with stamped chrysanthemum design

1312　元　青釉里刻花外模印莲瓣纹碗标本

Yuan dynasty

Specimen of green glaze bowl with incised design inside and moulded lotus-petal design outside

1313　元　青釉刻花花卉纹碗标本

Yuan dynasty

Specimen of green glaze bowl with incised floral design

1314　元　**青釉刻花花卉纹碗标本**
Yuan dynasty
Specimen of green glaze bowl with incised floral design

1315　元　**青釉刻花莲瓣纹碗标本**
Yuan dynasty　Specimen of green glaze bowl with incised lotus-petal design

1316　元　**青釉里刻花花卉纹外刻莲瓣纹碗标本**
Yuan dynasty
Specimen of green glaze bowl with incised floral design inside and lotus-petal design outside

1317　元　**青釉刻划花纹碗标本**
Yuan dynasty
Specimen of green glaze bowl with incised design

1318　元　**青釉刻划花篦划纹碗标本**

Yuan dynasty

Specimen of green glaze bowl with comb-incised design

1319　元　**青釉刻划花篦划纹碗标本**

Yuan dynasty

Specimen of green glaze bowl with comb-incised design

1320 **元　青釉刻划花篦划纹碗标本**

Yuan dynasty

Specimens of green glaze bowl with comb-incised design

1321　元　青釉刻划花篦划纹碗标本
Yuan dynasty
Specimens of green glaze bowl with comb-incised design

1322　元　青釉刻划花篦划纹碗标本
Yuan dynasty　Specimen of green glaze bowl with comb-incised design

1323　元　青釉里刻划花篦划纹外刻莲瓣纹碗标本

Yuan dynasty　Specimen of green glaze bowl with comb-incised design inside and incised lotus-petal design outside

1324　元　青釉划花纹碗标本

Yuan dynasty

Specimen of green glaze bowl with incised design

1325　元　青釉划花篦划纹碗标本
Yuan dynasty
Specimen of green glaze bowl with comb-incised design

1326　元　黑釉碗标本
Yuan dynasty
Specimen of black glaze bowl

1327 元 素胎印"郭山"铭碗标本

Yuan dynasty

Specimen of unglazed bowl with inscription of Chinese characters Guo Shan

1328 元 窑具标本

Yuan dynasty

Specimens of kiln furniture

1329 **元　窑具标本**
Yuan dynasty
Specimen of kiln furniture

1330 **元　窑具标本**
Yuan dynasty
Specimens of kiln furniture

# 云和窑

为元明时期瓷窑，共有窑址约20处。2009年故宫博物院部分专家学者调查了铁炉后与上孔青两处青瓷窑。

铁炉后窑。是一处烧造元代龙泉窑风格的瓷窑，器物造型以碗为多，此外还有炉、盘、高足杯等。造型与烧造工艺元代特征明显，其中一些器物有刻划花、印花装饰，刻花多见莲瓣纹，饰于碗外，也有的碗于外口沿刻划数道弦纹，再在弦纹上刻划竖条纹多组，看上去像简单的回纹，与龙泉大窑同类器物装饰相似。碗、盘内也有刻划简单的花卉纹的。印花多折枝团花、菊花、莲花等，与元代龙泉窑同类装饰近似。

上孔青窑。为龙窑，窑址有匣钵堆积，垫饼数量很多，少量青瓷标本。有花口、花式碗，据介绍还烧盘、高足杯等。釉有青、青黄、开片多种。装饰有划花、模印菊瓣纹等。足底心垫饼支烧，垫饼有大小高矮多种样式。

# Yunhe Kiln

Most of them are dated back to Yuan and Ming dynasty. There are about 20 kiln sites. Experts from the Palace Museum investigated kiln sites at Tieluhou and Shangkongqing in 2009.

Wares of Yuan dynasty Longquan kiln style were fired at Tieluhou. Among the wares fired, bowls are the largest in number, followed by burners, plates, cups with high stem, etc. Shaping and firing technique has clear characteristics of Yuan dynasty. Some of the wares are with incised or stamped design. The popular pattern incised is lotus-petal as outside decoration of bowl. Bowls with incised design of several strings along the rim outside and groups of vertical lines connecting the strings which look like simplified rectangular spiral patterns, are similar to that of Longquan kiln at Dayao. Bowls and plates are also with incised floral design in simplicity. Stamped patterns are medallion, chrysanthemum lotus, etc., very close to the decoration of the same kind of Longquan kiln in Yuan dynasty.

Kiln Shangkongqing used to be a dragon kiln. Saggars, pads in great numbers and a small number of parts of green glaze wares were among the accumulation at the kiln site. There are bowls either with flower rim or in shape of flower. It is said that the kiln also fired plates, cups with high stem, etc. Glaze is in green, greenish yellow and has crackles. Regarding decoration, the kiln used incised design and stamped design of molded chrysanthemum and so on. Wares were fired using pads against the bottom. Pads vary in size and height.

**云和（铁炉后）窑遗址**
Ruin of Yunhe kiln at Tieluhou

**云和（铁炉后）窑遗址**
Ruin of Yunhe kiln at Tieluhou

1331　**元　青釉三足炉标本**
Yuan dynasty
Specimen of green glaze burner with three-legged design

1332　**元　青釉碗标本**
Yuan dynasty
Specimen of green glaze bowl

1333　元　青釉碗标本

Yuan dynasty

Specimens of green glaze bowl

1334　元　**青釉碗标本**

Yuan dynasty

Specimens of green glaze bowl

1335 元 青釉碗标本

Yuan dynasty

Specimens of green glaze bowl

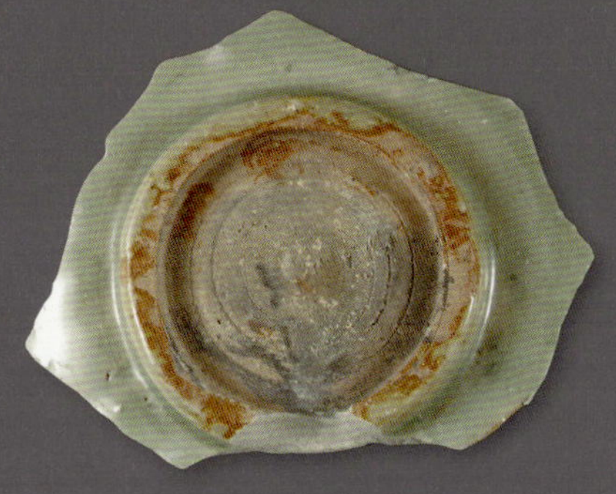
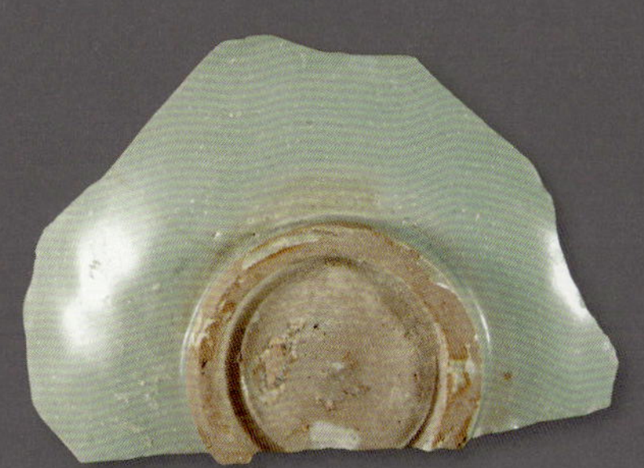

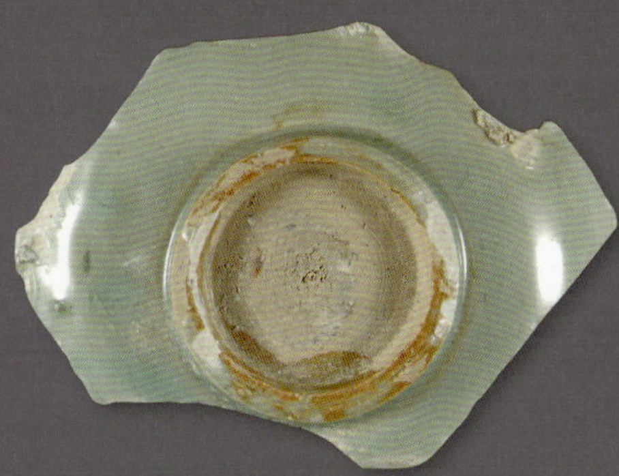

1336 **元 青釉盘标本**

Yuan dynasty

Specimens of green glaze plate

1337　元　**青釉折沿盘标本**

Yuan dynasty

Specimens of green glaze plate with everted flange

1338 **元　青釉印花莲花纹碗标本**

Yuan dynasty

Specimens of green glaze bowl with stamped lotus design

1339　**元　青釉印花莲花纹碗标本**

Yuan dynasty

Specimens of green glaze bowl with stamped lotus design

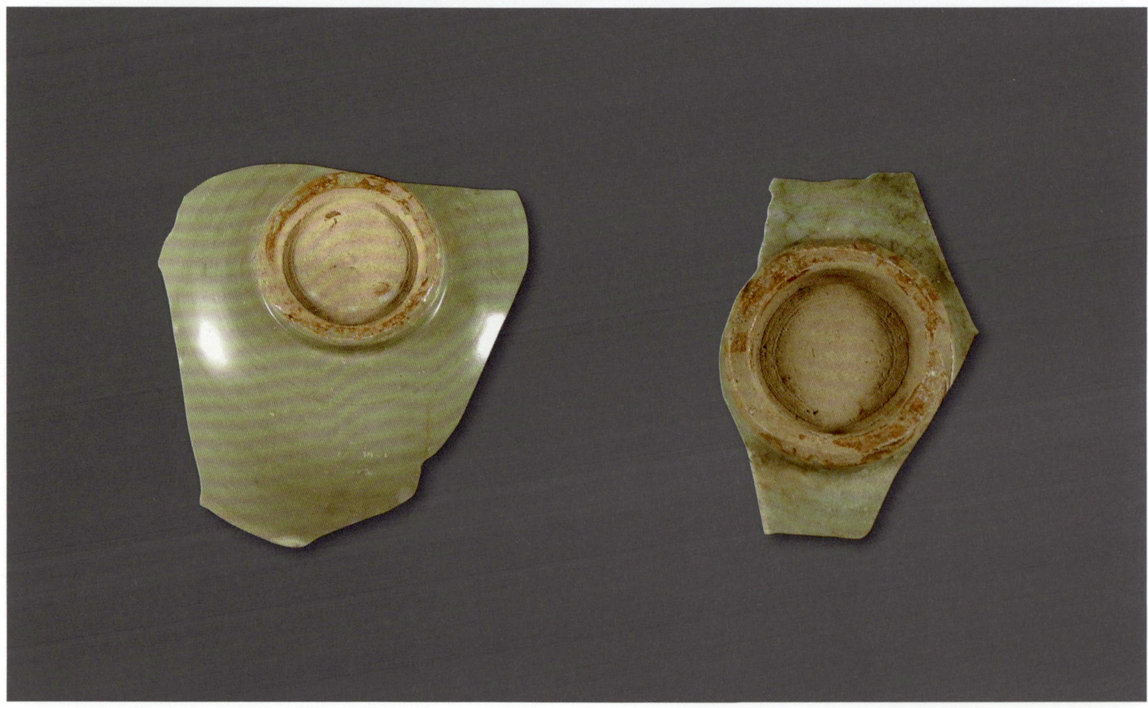

## 1340 元 青釉印花菊花纹碗标本

Yuan dynasty

Specimens of green glaze bowl with stamped chrysanthemum design

1341　元　**青釉印花菊花纹碗标本**

Yuan dynasty

Specimens of green glaze bowl with stamped chrysanthemum design

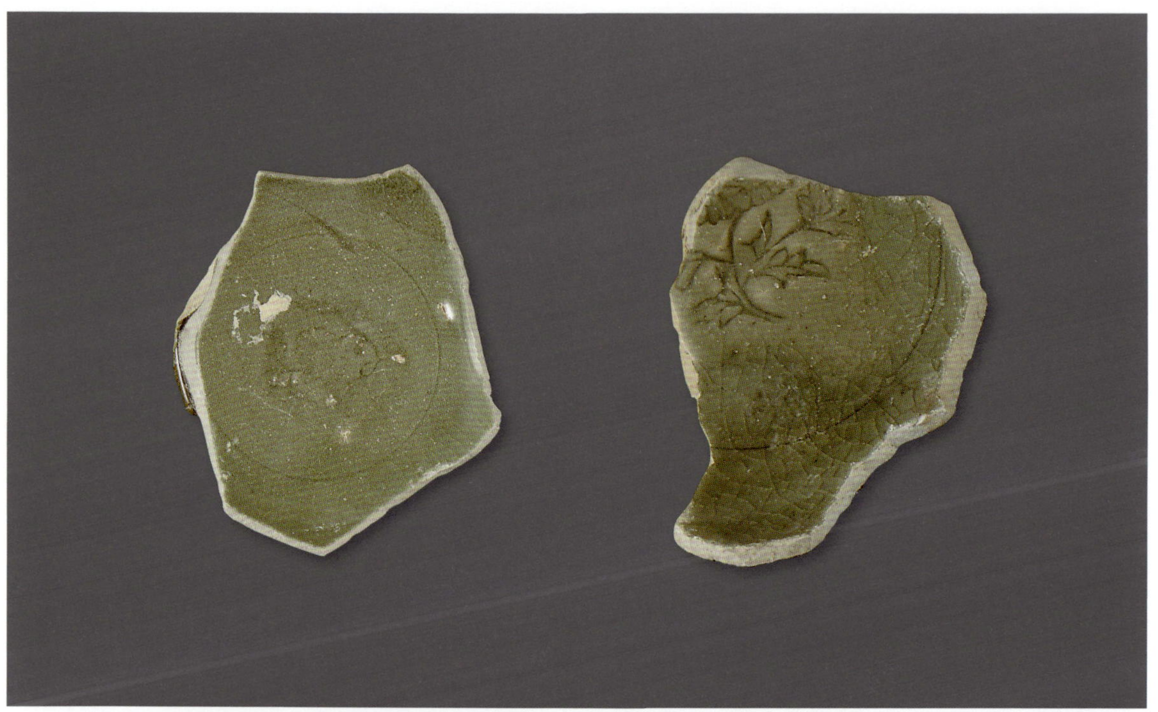

1342 **元　青釉印花鱼纹碗标本**

Yuan dynasty

Specimens of green glaze bowl with stamped fish design

1343 元 青釉印花莲花纹盘标本
Yuan dynasty
Specimens of green glaze plate with stamped lotus design

1344 元 青釉印花莲花纹盘标本
Yuan dynasty Specimen of green glaze plate with stamped lotus design

1345 元 青釉印花莲花纹高足杯标本
Yuan dynasty Specimen of green glaze cup with high stem and stamped lotus design

1346 元 青釉印花莲花纹高足杯标本

Yuan dynasty

Specimens of green glaze cup with high stem and stamped lotus design

1347　元　**青釉印花花卉纹洗标本**
Yuan dynasty
Specimen of green glaze washer with stamped floral design

1348　元　**青釉里印花菊花纹外刻花莲瓣纹碗标本**
Yuan dynasty
Specimen of green glaze bowl with stamped chrysanthemum design inside and incised louts-petal design outside

1349　元　**青釉里印花莲花纹外刻花花瓣纹高足杯标本**

Yuan dynasty

Specimen of green glaze cup with high stem and stamped lotus design inside and incised flower-petal design outside

1350　元　青釉里印花莲花纹外刻花花瓣纹高足杯标本

Yuan dynasty　Specimen of green glaze cup with high stem and stamped lotus design inside and incised flower-petal design outside

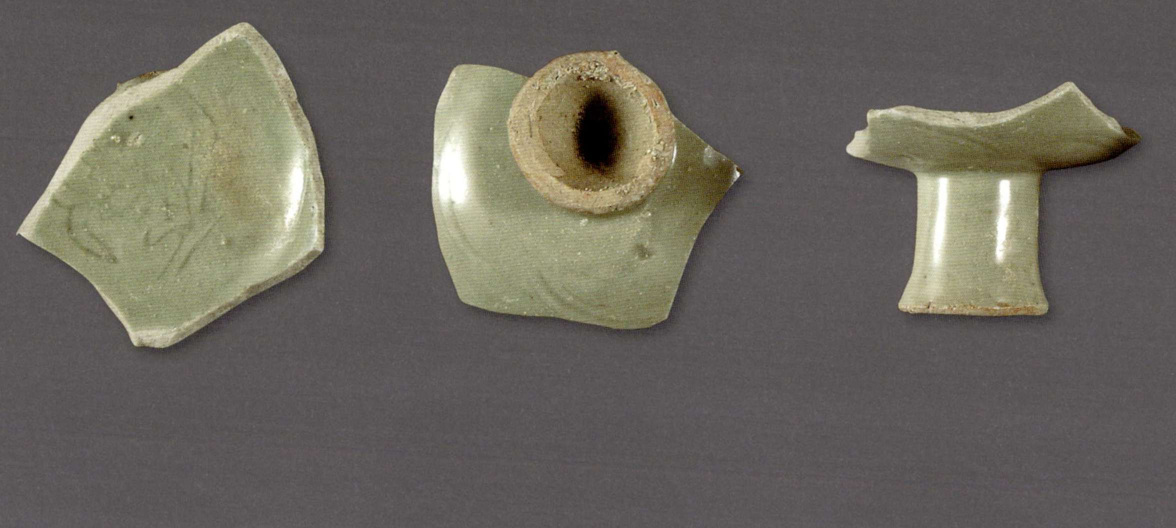

1351　元　青釉里印花菊花纹外刻花莲瓣纹高足杯标本

Yuan dynasty　Specimen of green glaze cup with high stem and stamped chrysanthemum design inside and incised lotus-petal design outside

1352　元　**青釉刻花莲瓣纹碗标本**

Yuan dynasty

Specimens of green glaze bowl with incised lotus-petal design

1353　**元　青釉刻弦纹碗标本**

Yuan dynasty

Specimens of green glaze bowl with incised string design

1354　元　青釉刻弦纹碗标本
Yuan dynasty　Specimen of green glaze bowl with incised string design

1355　元　青釉刻花莲瓣纹折沿盘标本
Yuan dynasty　Specimen of green glaze plate with everted flange and incised lotus-petal design

1356　元至明　青釉里划花外刻弦纹碗标本
From Yuan dynasty to Ming dynasty
Specimens of green glaze bowl with incised design inside and incised strings outside

1357　**元至明　窑具标本**

From Yuan dynasty to Ming dynasty

Specimens of kiln furniture

**云和（上孔青）窑遗址保护牌**

Monument for protecting the ruin of Yunhe kiln at Shangkongqing

**云和（上孔青）窑遗址瓷片遗存**

Pileup of porcelain parts at the ruin of Yunhe kiln at Shangkongqing

1358　元　青釉碗标本
Yuan dynasty
Specimen of green glaze bowl

1359　元　青釉盘标本
Yuan dynasty
Specimen of green glaze plate

1360　元　青釉模印菊瓣纹花式盘标本
Yuan dynasty
Specimen of green glaze flower-shaped plate with mould-stamped design of chrysanthemum-petal

1361　元　青釉刻划花碗标本
Yuan dynasty
Specimen of green glaze bowl with incised design

1362　元　窑具标本
Yuan dynasty
Specimens of kiln furniture

# 龙泉窑

窑址在浙江省龙泉县，遗址范围广大，故宫博物院部分专家学者20世纪50年代、70年代、80年代及2004年、2007年调查了龙泉山头、溪口、金村、大窑、上年儿、岭脚、碗圈山、杉树连山、落乌口、枫树坪官厂、安仁、前赖、梧桐口、瓯丽保等处窑址。

龙泉窑是宋代著名的青瓷窑之一，创烧于三国时期，北宋烧制具有自身特点的青瓷，南宋为其鼎盛时期，元代在烧制大件器物的技术上取得成功，明中期以后逐渐走向衰落，有一千多年的烧瓷历史。对邻近地区瓷窑影响较大，江西、福建、广东等省的一批瓷窑出现仿烧龙泉窑的产品。

龙泉窑北宋时多用刻花与篦划纹装饰。南宋时为宫廷烧造瓷器，胎体洁白，釉色葱绿，粉青与梅子青釉是当时的名贵品种，同时仿烧官窑黑胎青瓷，造型多仿古代青铜器、玉器式样。元代印花装饰有所发展，以印纹为多，贴花装饰亦比较流行，以鱼纹、缠枝花纹为多，龙纹也有一定数量。素胎贴花是元代龙泉窑经常使用的装饰方法之一。在瓶、盘、洗等器物上模印贴花，花纹露胎，不施釉，与花纹以外的青釉形成鲜明对比。常见纹饰有鱼、花卉、龙纹等。明代初年与景德镇窑一起为宫廷烧制御用瓷器，青釉色泽深绿匀净，玻璃质感强，造型、装饰花纹与景德镇青花具有共同风格。

# Longquan Kiln

Longquan kiln is located in Longquan County, Zhejiang Province. Its kiln sites are vastly distributed across the county. Experts from the Palace Museum investigated kiln sites at Shantou, Xikou, Jincun, Dayao, Shangnianer, Lingjiao, Wanquanshan, Shanshulianshan, Luoniaokou, Fengshupingguanchang, Anren, Qianlai, Wutongkou, Oulibao, etc. in the 1950s, 1970s, 1980s and in 2004 and 2007.

Longquan kiln was one of the famous celadon kilns in Song dynasty. It started to fire in Three Kingdoms. Celadon with its own characteristics was fired in Northern Song dynasty. The kiln reached its heyday in Southern Song dynasty. It succeeded in firing large size pieces in Yuan dynasty. After mid-Ming dynasty, it gradually went fade. With a firing history of over one thousand years, it had an important impact on kilns in Jiangxi, Fujian, Guangdong and other provinces. Those kilns imitated products of Longquan kiln.

In Northern Song dynasty, Longquan kiln wares were usually with incised design. In Southern Song dynasty, it fired green glaze wares of white body and light green glaze for the imperial court. Of which, light greenish blue and plum green were rare and valuable. In the mean time, it imitated green glaze wares with black body of Guan kiln. The imitated ones most often took the shape of ancient bronze and jade wares. Great achievements were witnessed in Yuan dynasty in the decoration of green glaze wares with stamped design. Celadon decoration with applied design is also popular. The frequently used patterns in applied design are fish, interlocking flowers and dragons under certain circumstance. Unglazed with applied design was one of the frequently used decorative methods of Longquan kiln in Yuan dynasty. Wares such as vases, plates, washers, etc. were with applied design of molded patterns with no glaze, making them a striking contrast to the rest of celadon. Common molded patterns are fish, flowers, dragons, etc. In early Ming dynasty, the kiln, together with Jingdezhen kiln, fired tribute porcelains for the imperial court. The tribute celadon was evenly glazed in dark green and strongly glassy. Shaping and decorative patterns are the same as that of blue and white wares of Jingdezhen kiln.

1363 **北宋**

**青釉“雍熙二年”铭瓷板标本**

Northern Song dynasty

Specimen of green glaze board with inscription of Chinese characters Yong Xi Er Nian

1364 **宋 青釉刻花花卉纹碗标本**

Song dynasty

Specimen of green glaze bowl with incised floral design

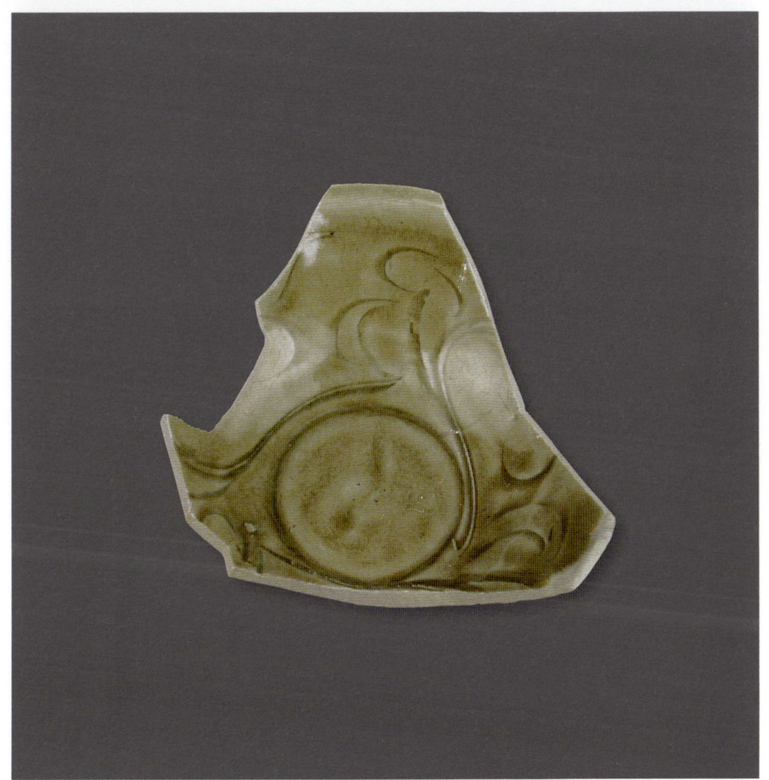

1365　**宋　青釉刻花分格花卉纹碗标本**

Song dynasty

Specimen of green glaze bowl with incised flower design on panels

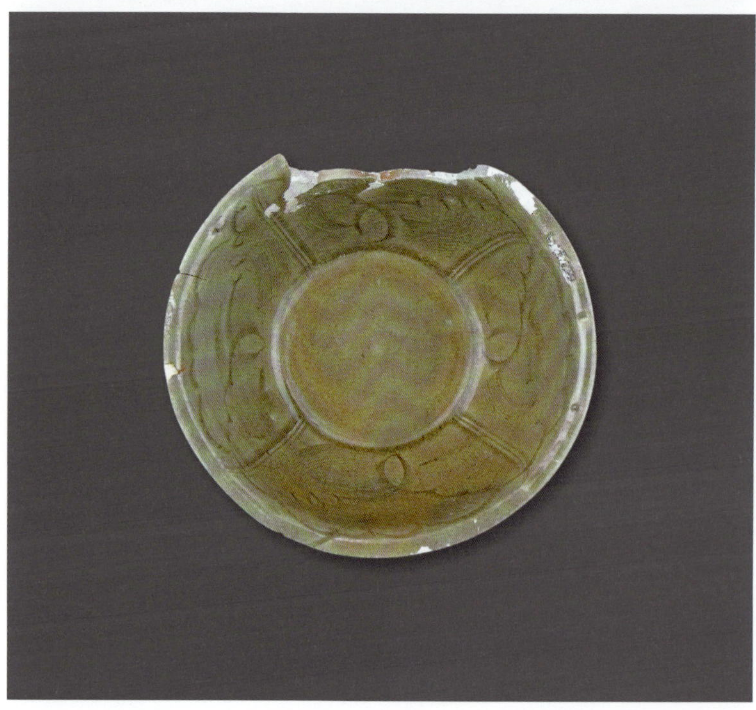

1366　**宋**

**青釉刻花分格花卉纹碗标本**

Song dynasty

Specimen of green glaze bowl with incised floral design on panels

1367　宋　**青釉里刻花分格花卉纹外刻花莲瓣纹碗标本**
Song dynasty
Specimen of green glaze bowl with incised flower design on panels inside and lotus-petal design outside

1368　宋　**青釉里刻花分格花卉纹外刻花莲瓣纹碗标本**
Song dynasty
Specimen of green glaze bowl with incised flower design on panels inside and lotus-petal design outside

1369 **宋　青釉里刻花荷叶纹外刻线纹碗标本**

Song dynasty

Specimen of green glaze bowl with incised lotus-leaf design inside and incised line design outside

1370 **宋　青釉刻花篦划莲花纹碗标本**

Song dynasty

Specimen of green glaze bowl with comb-incised lotus design

1371　宋　青釉刻花篦划莲花纹碗标本
Song dynasty
Specimens of green glaze bowl with comb-incised lotus design

1372　宋　青釉里刻花篦划花卉纹外刻线纹碗标本
Song dynasty
Specimen of green glaze bowl with comb-incised floral design inside and incised line design outside

1373 **宋 青釉里刻花篦划花卉纹外刻线纹碗标本**

Song dynasty

Specimen of green glaze bowl with comb-incised floral design inside and incised line design outside

1374 **宋 青釉里刻花篦划双鱼纹外刻线纹碗标本**

Song dynasty

Specimen of green glaze bowl with comb-incised pair fish design inside and incised line design outside

1375 **宋 青釉刻花篦划荷莲纹盘标本**

Song dynasty

Specimens of green glaze plate with comb-incised lotus design

1376 **宋**
**青釉刻花篦划荷莲纹盘标本**
Song dynasty
Specimen of green glaze plate with comb-incised lotus design

1377 **宋 青釉里刻花篦划花卉纹外刻划花莲瓣纹碗标本**
Song dynasty
Specimen of green glaze bowl with comb-incised flower design inside and incised lotus-petal design outside

1378 **宋　青釉刻划花莲瓣纹炉标本**
Song dynasty
Specimens of green glaze burner with incised lotus-petal design

1379 **宋**
**青釉刻划花篦划花卉纹碗标本**
Song dynasty
Specimen of green glaze bowl
with comb-incised floral design

1380　宋　青釉刻划花篦划荷莲纹碗标本

Song dynasty

Specimen of green glaze bowl with comb-incised lotus design

1381 **宋　青釉刻划花篦划花叶纹盘标本**
Song dynasty　Specimen of green glaze plate with comb-incised flower and leaf design

1382 **宋　青釉划花篦划纹盘标本**
Song dynasty　Specimen of green glaze plate with comb-incised design

**龙泉（溪口）窑遗址外景**
Ruin of Longquan kiln at Xikou

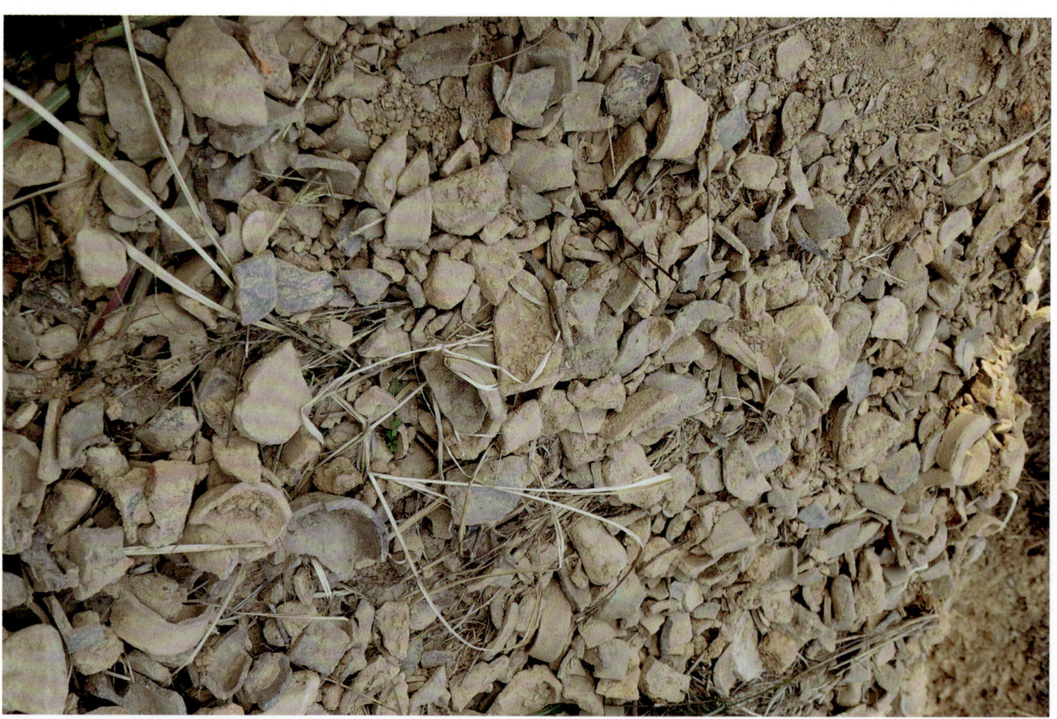

**龙泉（溪口）窑遗址瓷片遗存**
Pileup of porcelain parts at the ruin of Longquan kiln at Xikou

1383 **宋　青釉瓶标本**

Song dynasty

Specimens of green glaze vase

1384　**宋　青釉瓶标本**

Song dynasty

Specimens of green glaze vase

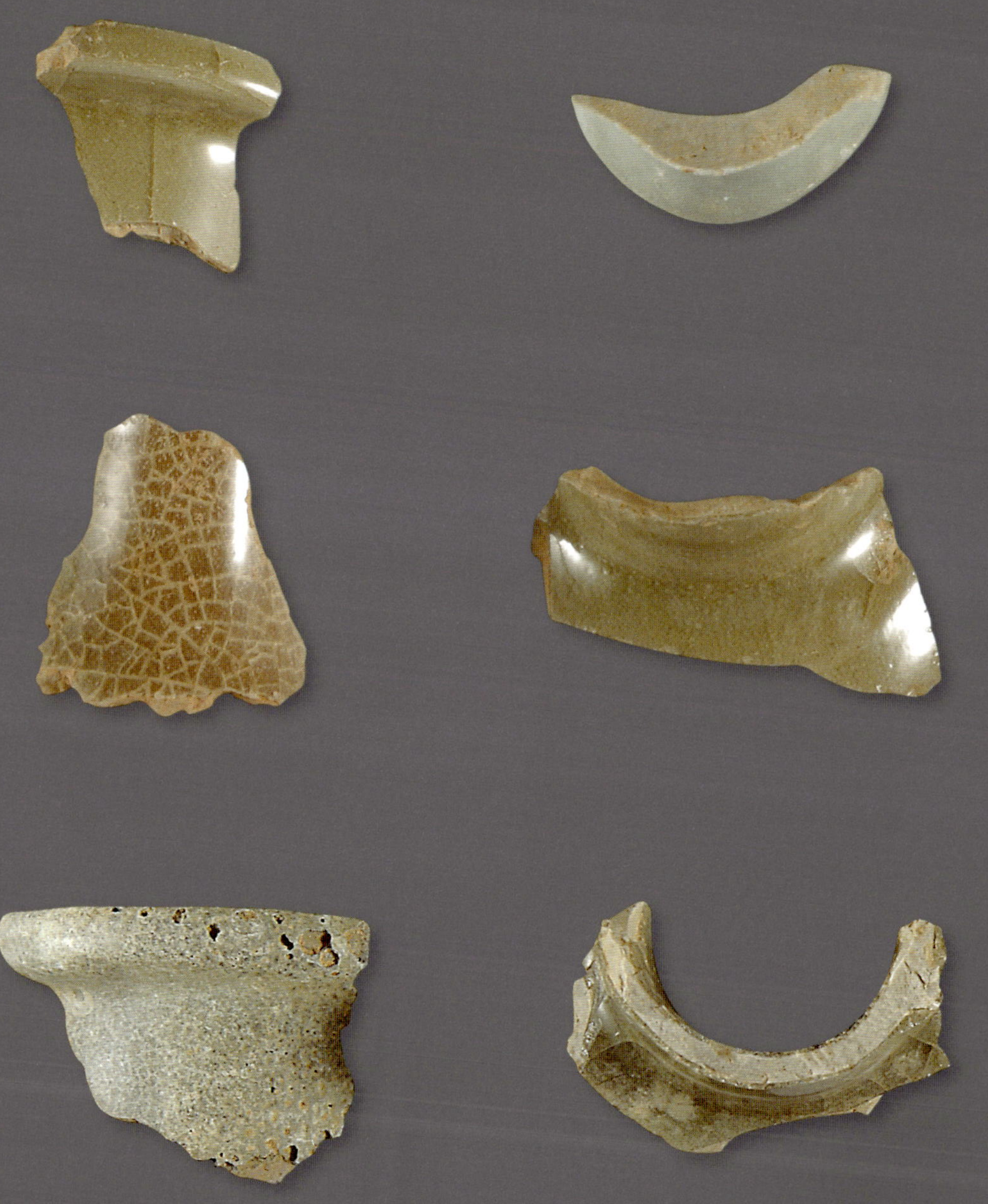

1385 宋 青釉瓶标本
Song dynasty
Specimen of green glaze vase

1386 宋 青釉花式瓶标本
Song dynasty
Specimen of green glaze flower-shaped vase

1387　宋　青釉筒式炉标本
Song dynasty
Specimens of green glaze barrel-shaped burner

1388　宋　青釉三足炉标本
Song dynasty
Specimens of green glaze burner with three-legged design

1389 **宋　青釉三足炉标本**

Song dynasty

Specimens of green glaze burner with three-legged design

1390 **宋 青釉三足炉标本**

Song dynasty

Specimens of green glaze burner with three-legged design

1391 **宋 青釉三足炉标本**
Song dynasty Specimens of green glaze burner with three-legged design

1392 **宋 青釉三足炉标本**
Song dynasty Specimens of green glaze burner with three-legged design

1393 **宋　青釉出戟三足炉标本**
Song dynasty
Specimen of green glaze burner
with ribs and three-legged design

1394 **宋　青釉出戟三足炉标本**
Song dynasty
Specimens of green glaze burner
with ribs and three-legged design

1395 **宋　青釉器盖标本**
Song dynasty
Specimens of green glaze cover

1396 **宋　青釉器盖标本**
Song dynasty
Specimens of green glaze cover

1397 **宋 青釉器盖标本**
Song dynasty
Specimen of green glaze cover

1398 **宋 青釉匜标本**
Song dynasty
Specimen of green glaze ewer

1399 **宋 青釉碗标本**

Song dynasty

Specimens of green glaze bowl

1400 **宋　青釉碗标本**

Song dynasty

Specimens of green glaze bowl

1401 **宋　青釉碗标本**

Song dynasty

Specimens of green glaze bowl

1402 **宋　青釉碗标本**

Song dynasty

Specimens of green glaze bowl

1403 **宋　青釉碗标本**

Song dynasty

Specimens of green glaze bowl

1404 **宋　青釉盘标本**
Song dynasty
Specimens of green glaze plate

1405　宋　青釉盘标本
Song dynasty
Specimens of green glaze plate

1406 **宋 青釉盘标本**
Song dynasty
Specimen of green glaze plate

1407 **宋 青釉折沿盘标本**
Song dynasty
Specimen of green glaze plate with everted flange

1408　**宋　青釉八方折沿盘标本**

Song dynasty

Specimens of green glaze eight-sided plate with everted flange

1409 **宋　青釉弦纹筒式炉标本**
Song dynasty
Specimens of green glaze barrel-shaped burner with design of strings

1410 **宋　青釉印花花卉纹罐标本**
Song dynasty
Specimen of green glaze jar with
stamped floral design

1411 **宋 青釉印花莲瓣纹罐标本**
Song dynasty
Specimen of green glaze jar with stamped lotus-petal design

1412 **宋 青釉印花碗标本**
Song dynasty
Specimen of green glaze bowl with stamped design

1413 **宋 青釉印花莲瓣纹碗标本**
Song dynasty
Specimen of green glaze bowl with stamped lotus-petal design

1414 **宋 青釉刻线纹罐标本**
Song dynasty
Specimen of green glaze jar with incised line design

1415　**宋　青釉刻划花莲瓣纹碗标本**
Song dynasty
Specimens of green glaze bowl with incised lotus-petal design

1416　**宋　青釉贴花筒式炉标本**
Song dynasty
Specimen of green glaze barrel-shaped burner with stamped design

1417 **宋至元　青釉模印菊瓣式碗标本**

From Song dynasty to Yuan dynasty

Specimens of green glaze chrysanthemum-petal-shaped bowl

1418 **宋至元　青釉模印菊瓣式碗标本**

From Song dynasty to Yuan dynasty

Specimens of green glaze chrysanthemum-petal-shaped bowl

1419　**南宋至元**

**青釉印花环耳瓶标本**

From Southern Song dynasty to Yuan dynasty

Specimen of green glaze vase with ring-shaped handles and stamped design

1420　**元　青釉高足杯标本**

Yuan dynasty

Specimen of green glaze cup with high stem

1421　**宋至元　窑具标本**

From Song dynasty to Yuan dynasty

Specimen of kiln furniture

1422 宋至元 窑具标本

From Song dynasty to Yuan dynasty

Specimens of kiln furniture

## 1423 南宋　青釉花口碗标本

Southern Song dynasty

Specimens of green glaze bowl with flower rim

1424 **南宋 青釉折沿盘标本**
Southern Song dynasty
Specimens of green glaze plate with everted flange

1425 **南宋**
**青釉弦纹壶（瓶）标本**
Southern Song dynasty
Specimen of green glaze pot (vase)
with design of strings

1426　**南宋　青釉印“金玉满堂”铭花口碗标本**

Southern Song dynasty　Specimen of green glaze bowl with flower rim and inscription of Chinese characters Jin Yu Man Tang

1427　**南宋　青釉印花花卉纹盘标本**

Southern Song dynasty　Specimen of green glaze plate with stamped floral design

1428　**南宋　青釉印花双鱼纹洗标本**
Southern Song dynasty
Specimen of green glaze washer with stamped pair fish design

1429　**南宋　青釉印花双鱼纹折沿洗标本**
Southern Song dynasty
Specimen of green glaze washer with everted flange and stamped pair fish design

1430　**南宋　青釉刻花菊瓣纹碗标本**

Southern Song dynasty

Specimens of green glaze bowl with incised chrysanthemum-petal design

1431　**南宋**

**青釉刻花菊瓣纹碗标本**

Southern Song dynasty

Specimen of green glaze bowl with incised chrysanthemum-petal design

1432 **南宋 青釉里刻花篦划纹外刻花莲瓣纹碗标本**

Southern Song dynasty

Specimen of green glaze bowl with comb-incised design inside and incised louts-petal design outside

1433 **南宋 青釉刻花莲花纹盘标本**

Southern Song dynasty

Specimen of green glaze plate with incised lotus design

1434　**南宋　青釉刻花莲花纹盘标本**

Southern Song dynasty

Specimens of green glaze plate with incised lotus design

1435　**南宋　青釉刻花菊瓣纹盘标本**

Southern Song dynasty

Specimen of green glaze plate with incised chrysanthemum-petal design

1436　**南宋　青釉刻花菊瓣纹盘标本**
Southern Song dynasty　Specimen of green glaze plate with incised chrysanthemum-petal design

1437　**南宋　青釉刻花篦划纹折沿盘标本**
Southern Song dynasty　Specimen of green glaze plate with comb-incised design and everted flange

1438 **南宋　青釉刻划花荷莲纹碗标本**

Southern Song dynasty

Specimens of green glaze bowl with incised lotus design

1439 **南宋**

**青釉刻划花荷莲纹碗标本**

Southern Song dynasty

Specimen of green glaze bowl with incised lotus design

1440 **南宋**

**青釉刻划花荷莲纹碗标本**

Southern Song dynasty

Specimen of green glaze bowl with incised lotus design

1441　**南宋　青釉刻划花篦划花卉纹碗标本**

Southern Song dynasty

Specimen of green glaze bowl with comb-incised floral design

1442　**南宋　青釉刻划花篦划鱼纹碗标本**

Southern Song dynasty

Specimen of green glaze bowl with comb-incised fish design

1443　**南宋　青釉刻划花篦点团菊纹碗标本**
Southern Song dynasty
Specimen of green glaze bowl with comb-incised design of dots and medallion of chrysanthemum

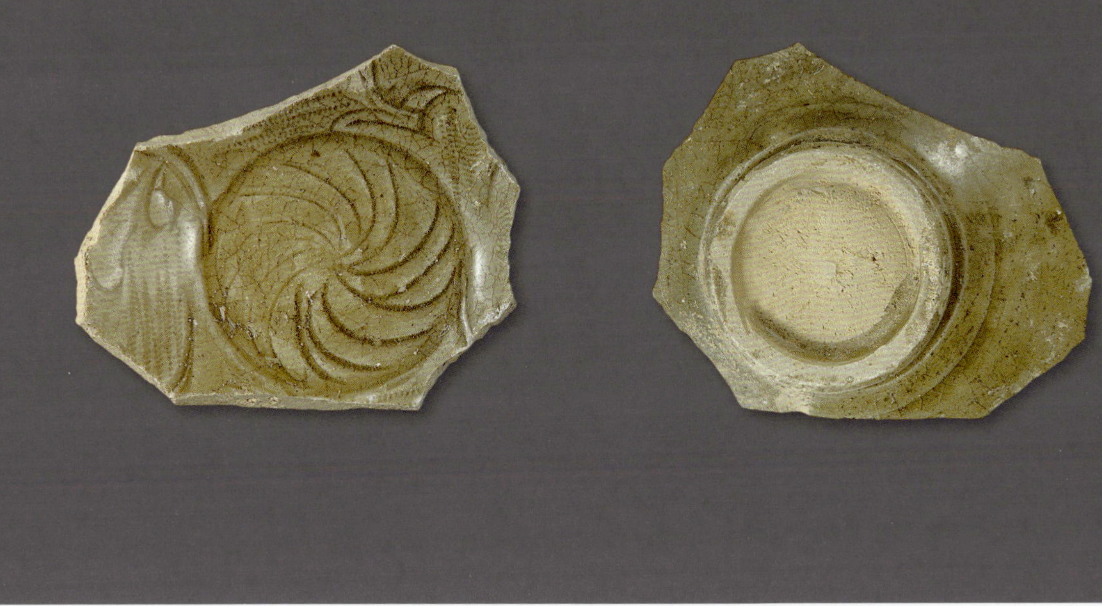

1444　**南宋　青釉刻划花莲瓣纹供碗标本**
Southern Song dynasty
Specimens of green glaze sacrificial bowl with incised lotus-petal design

1445　南宋　青釉划花花瓣纹花口碗标本

Southern Song dynasty

Specimens of green glaze bowl with flower rim and incised flower-petal design

1446　**南宋　青釉划花花瓣纹花口碗标本**

Southern Song dynasty

Specimens of green glaze bowl with flower rim and incised flower-petal design

1447 **南宋 青釉划花篦划纹碗标本**
Southern Song dynasty Specimen of green glaze bowl with comb-incised design

1448 **南宋至元 青釉刻花花卉纹碗标本**
From Southern Song dynasty to Yuan dynasty
Specimen of green glaze bowl with incised floral design

1449 **南宋至元　青釉刻花荷莲纹碗标本**

From Southern Song dynasty to Yuan dynasty

Specimens of green glaze bowl with incised lotus design

1450 **南宋至元 青釉刻划花花卉纹碗标本**
From Southern Song dynasty to Yuan dynasty
Specimen of green glaze bowl with incised floral design

1451 **南宋 窑具标本**
Southern Song dynasty
Specimen of kiln furniture

1452 **南宋 窑具标本**
Southern Song dynasty
Specimen of kiln furniture

**龙泉大窑遗址**
Ruin of Longquan kiln at Dayao

**龙泉大窑遗址瓷片遗存**
Pileup of porcelain parts at the ruin of Longquan kiln at Dayao

## 1453 南宋　青釉贯耳瓶标本

Southern Song dynasty

Specimen of green glaze vase with pierced handles

附图

**南宋　青釉贯耳八方瓶**

高 12.9 厘米
口径 5.1 厘米 ×3.7 厘米
足径 5.2 厘米 ×4.2 厘米
故宫博物院藏

Illustration
Southern Song dynasty
Green glaze octagonal vase with pierced handles

Height 12.9cm, mouth size 5.1cm×3.7cm, foot size 5.2cm×4.2cm
Collected by the Palace Museum

瓶呈八方形，直口，长颈，溜肩，垂腹，圈足，近口处置双贯耳。灰白胎，施粉青釉，器身转折处釉色稍淡。圈足底边无釉，呈赭红色。

此贯耳瓶属于陈设用瓷，宋代开始流行。这种造型来源于汉代的投壶，当时的投壶多为青铜制作，也有漆器。宋代仿古风气盛行，陶瓷贯耳瓶除龙泉窑烧制外，官窑产品也很常见。

1454　**南宋　青釉贯耳瓶标本**
Southern Song dynasty
Specimen of green glaze vase with pierced handles

1455　**南宋　青釉壶标本**
Southern Song dynasty
Specimen of green glaze pot

1456　**南宋　青釉三足炉标本**

Southern Song dynasty

Specimens of green glaze burner with three-legged design

附图

**南宋　青釉三足炉**

高 4 厘米　口径 7.9 厘米
足距 5.2 厘米
故宫博物院藏

Illustration
Southern Song dynasty
Green glaze burner with three-legged design

Height 4cm, mouth diameter 7.9cm,
leg distance 5.2cm
Collected by the Palace Museum

炉直口，圆唇，筒形腹，平底置矮圈足，下承三兽形足。灰白胎。通体施青釉，釉面开片较大。

此炉圈足和三个兽形足兼具，这是龙泉窑筒式炉的一个特点。宋代时，三兽足对炉身起主要支撑作用，圈足通常不着地；到元代，一部分炉的圈足较高直接着地，而三兽足悬空，仅成为一种装饰。

1457 **南宋　青釉碗标本**
Southern Song dynasty
Specimen of green glaze bowl

1458 **南宋　青釉折沿洗标本**
Southern Song dynasty
Specimen of green glaze washer with everted flange

1459　**南宋　青釉折沿洗标本**
Southern Song dynasty
Specimens of green glaze washer with everted flange

1460　**南宋　青釉花口洗标本**
Southern Song dynasty
Specimen of green glaze washer
with flower rim

1461 **南宋　青釉琮式瓶标本**
Southern Song dynasty
Specimen of green glaze Cong-shaped vase

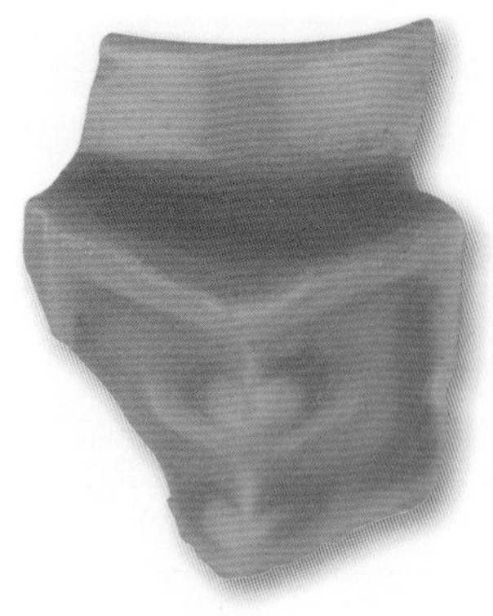

附图

**南宋　青釉琮式瓶**

高 25.2 厘米　口径 6.2 厘米
足径 6 厘米
故宫博物院藏

Illustration
Southern Song dynasty
Green glaze Cong-shaped vase

Height 25.2cm, mouth diameter 6.2cm,
foot diameter 6cm
Collected by the Palace Museum

瓶敛口，短颈，方柱形身，圈足。灰白胎。施梅子青釉，圈足底边无釉，呈淡赭红色。器身四面饰凸起横直条纹，纹饰凸起处釉色稍淡。

琮式瓶是仿玉琮制作的陈设用瓷。玉琮是古代重要礼器之一，内圆外方代表天和地，中间的穿孔代表天地之间的沟通，寓意“天圆地方、天地一统”。玉琮在新石器时代已大量出现，到宋代，仿古盛行，龙泉窑青瓷釉色青翠、釉质莹润，因此成为仿玉制品的最佳选择。

1462　南宋　青釉印花八卦纹炉标本

Southern Song dynasty

Specimen of green glaze burner with stamped design of eight divinatory trigrams

附图

**南宋　青釉印花八卦纹三足炉**

高 9 厘米　口径 14 厘米

底径 12 厘米

河北省文物总店藏

Illustration

Southern Song dynasty

Green glaze burner with stamped design of eight divinatory trigrams and three legs

Height 9cm, mouth diameter 14cm, bottom diameter 12cm

Collected by the Flag Antique Shop of Hebei Province

炉口内折，平底，底心有圆饼形足，外有三足。炉身上下各饰一条凸弦纹，弦纹间印阳纹八卦。

这种饼足与三足共同在一件器物上的做法元代较为流行，有的三足落地，有的三足悬空，为这一时期的特点。

1463 **南宋　青釉印花朵花纹碗标本**
Southern Song dynasty
Specimen of green glaze bowl with stamped flower design

1464 **南宋　青釉印花双鱼纹洗标本**
Southern Song dynasty
Specimen of green glaze washer with stamped pair fish design

附图

## 南宋　青釉印花双鱼纹折沿洗

高 6 厘米　口径 23.5 厘米
足径 13 厘米
故宫博物院藏

Illustration
Southern Song dynasty
Green glaze washer with stamped pair fish design and everted flange

Height 6cm, mouth diameter 23.5cm,
foot diameter 13cm
Collected by the Palace Museum

洗敞口，平折沿，折沿上对称开四孔，浅弧腹，圈足。灰白胎。通体施青釉，足底端无釉，呈浅赭红色。外壁装饰莲瓣纹一周，内底有弦纹二道，底心贴饰模印脊背相向的双鱼纹。

鱼纹作为陶瓷装饰，早在新石器时代的彩陶上就已出现。“鱼”与“余”同音，在民间常以鱼借喻生活富足有余；同时，由于鱼产子多，故也常用于祈吉求子，作为生育繁衍的象征。

1465　**南宋　青釉印花双鱼纹洗标本**

Southern Song dynasty

Specimen of green glaze washer with stamped pair fish design

1466　南宋　青釉里印花双鱼纹外刻花莲瓣纹洗标本

Southern Song dynasty

Specimen of green glaze washer with stamped pair fish design inside and incised lotus-petal design outside

1467　南宋　青釉里印花双鱼纹外刻花莲瓣纹折沿洗标本

Southern Song dynasty

Specimen of green glaze washer with everted flange and stamped pair fish design inside and incised lotus-petal design outside

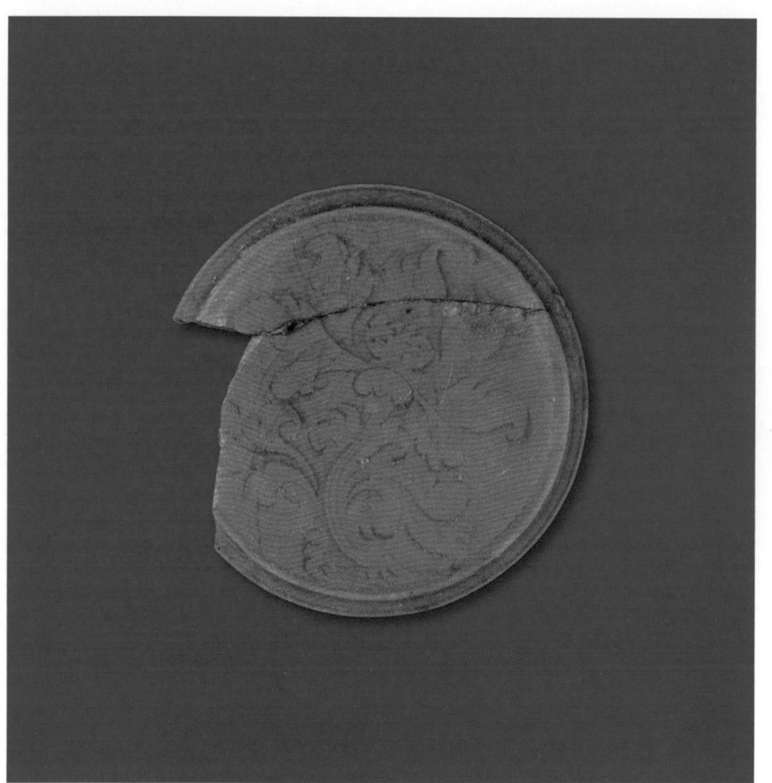

1468　南宋

**青釉刻花牡丹纹盒标本**

Southern Song dynasty

Specimen of green glaze box with incised peony design

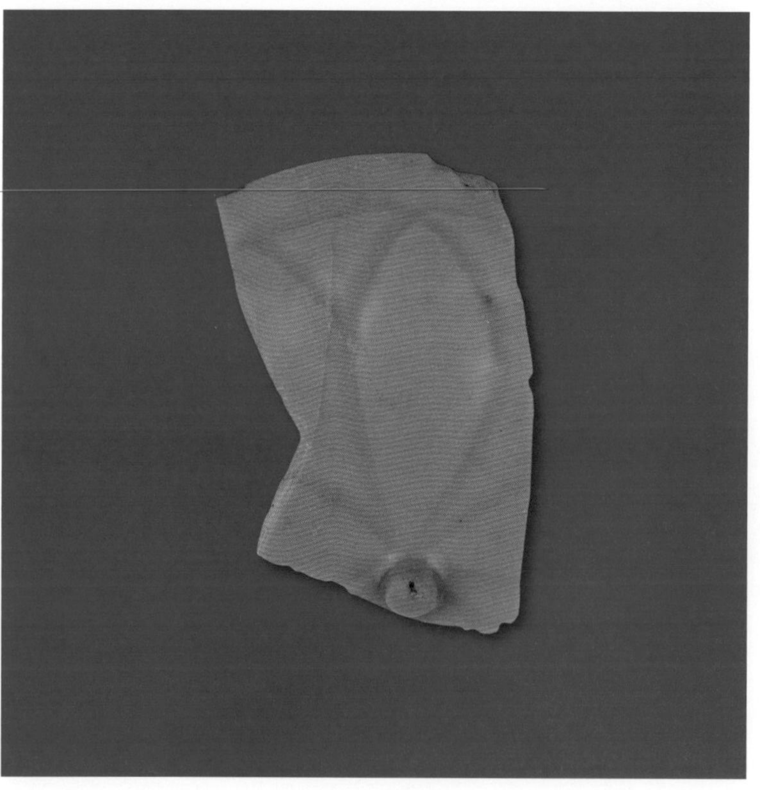

1469　南宋

**青釉刻花莲瓣纹器盖标本**

Southern Song dynasty

Specimen of green glaze cover with incised lotus-petal design

1470 **南宋**

**青釉刻花莲瓣纹碗标本**

Southern Song dynasty

Specimen of green glaze bowl

with incised lotus-petal design

1471 **南宋**

**青釉刻花莲瓣纹碗标本**

Southern Song dynasty

Specimens of green glaze bowl

with incised lotus-petal design

1472 **南宋 青釉刻花荷叶纹花口碗标本**
Southern Song dynasty
Specimen of green glaze bowl with flower rim and incised lotus-leaf design

1473 **南宋**
**青釉刻花莲瓣纹折沿洗标本**
Southern Song dynasty
Specimen of green glaze washer with everted flange and incised lotus-petal design

1474 **南宋 青釉仿官出戟炉标本**
Southern Song dynasty
Specimen of green glaze burner with ribs, imitation of Guan kiln

附图

**南宋 青釉仿官出戟三足炉**

高 5.2 厘米 口径 8 厘米
底径 4 厘米
故宫博物院藏

Illustration
Southern Song dynasty
Green glaze burner with three-legged design and ribs, imitation of Guan kiln

Height 5.2cm, mouth diameter 8cm,
bottom diameter 4cm
Collected by the Palace Museum

炉折沿，束颈，浅腹，下承以三足，三足内敛。肩部饰凸弦纹一道，三足上方各出一条状装饰，与足相连，比一般出戟三足炉出筋要粗得多。黑色胎，施青灰釉，釉面有开片。从造型、胎色到釉色均仿南宋官窑特征。

1475 **南宋 青釉仿官盘标本**
Southern Song dynasty
Specimen of green glaze plate, imitation of Guan kiln

1476 **南宋 青釉仿官盘标本**
Southern Song dynasty
Specimen of green glaze plate, imitation of Guan kiln

1477　**南宋至元　青釉模印菊瓣式洗标本**
From Southern Song dynasty to Yuan dynasty
Specimen of green glaze chrysanthemum-petal-shaped washer

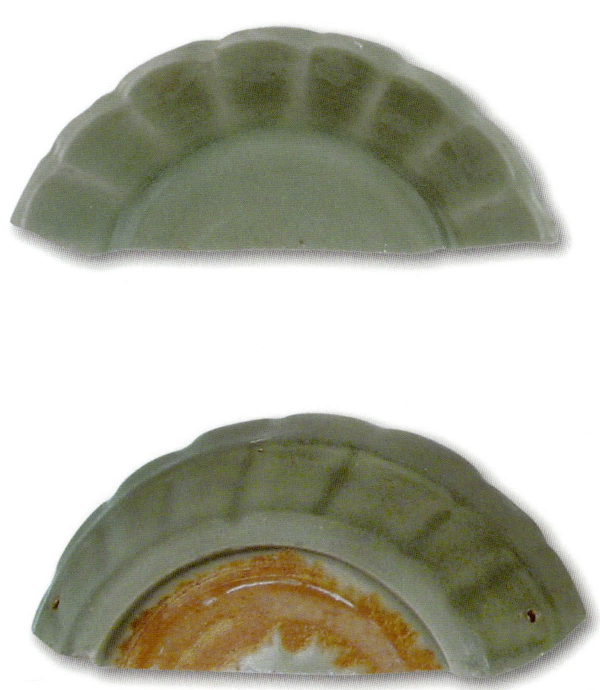

1478　**南宋至元　青釉模印菊瓣式洗标本**
From Southern Song dynasty to Yuan dynasty
Specimen of green glaze chrysanthemum-petal-shaped washer

1479　**元　青釉壶标本**

Yuan dynasty

Specimen of green glaze pot

附图

**明　青釉壶**

高 30 厘米　口径 8.4 厘米
足径 9.3 厘米
故宫博物院藏

Illustration
Ming dynasty　Green glaze pot

Height 30cm, mouth diameter 8.4cm,
foot diameter 9.3cm
Collected by the Palace Museum

壶身呈玉壶春瓶式，喇叭口，口沿微翻，圆唇，长颈，溜肩，圆腹，圈足。左右对称置高曲柄和长流，流与颈之间以云纹板相连。灰白胎，胎质坚密。釉色青绿，釉面光洁。外底无釉，呈赭红色。

1480 **元 青釉三足炉标本**
Yuan dynasty
Specimens of green glaze burner with three-legged design

1481 **元 青釉器盖标本**
Yuan dynasty
Specimen of green glaze cover

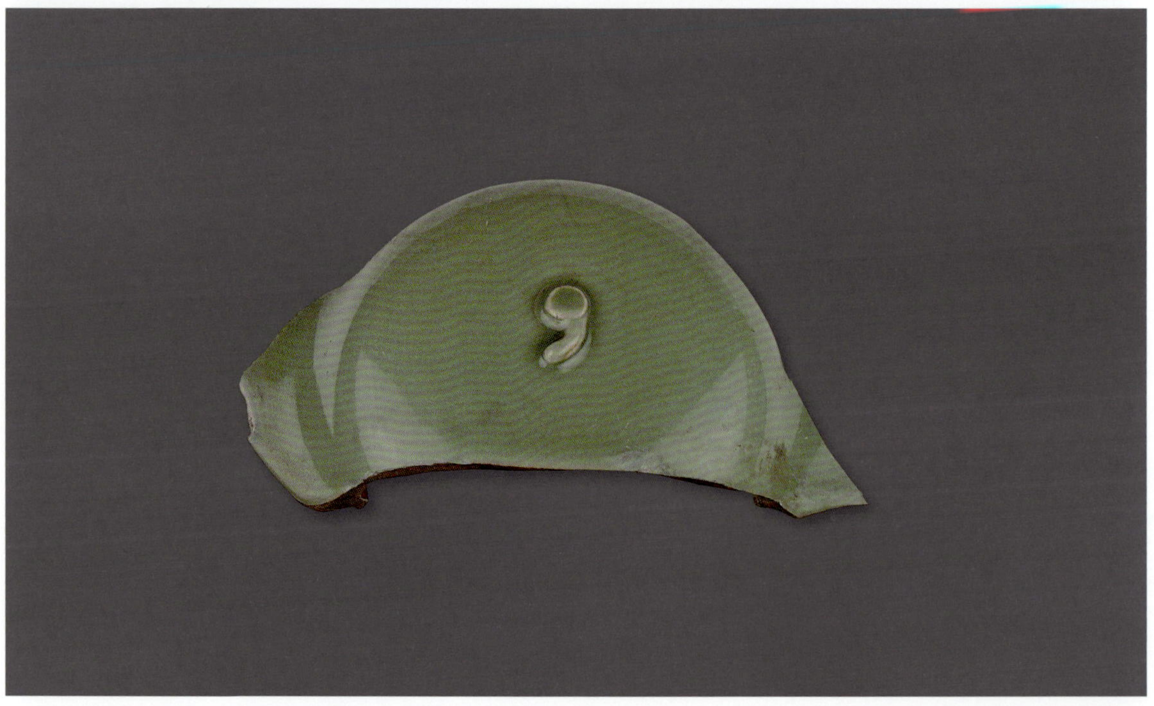

1482 元 青釉盘标本
Yuan dynasty
Specimen of green glaze plate

1483 元 青釉折沿盘标本
Yuan dynasty
Specimen of green glaze plate with everted flange

1484　元　**青釉印花花卉纹瓶标本**

Yuan dynasty

Specimen of green glaze vase with stamped floral design

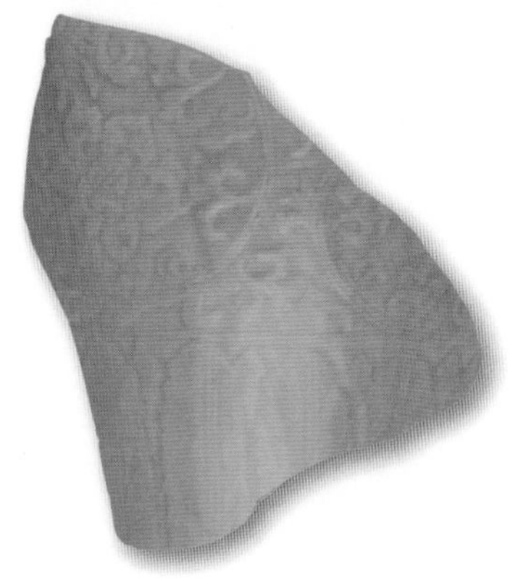

附图

**元　青釉印花花卉纹尊**

高 72 厘米　口径 33 厘米
足径 20.5 厘米
故宫博物院藏

Illustration

Yuan dynasty　Green glaze Zun vase with stamped floral design

Height 72cm, mouth diameter 33cm,
foot diameter 20.5cm
Collected by the Palace Museum

尊撇口，长颈，丰肩，鼓腹，下腹微收，圈足。灰白胎，通体施青釉。圈足底端无釉，呈浅赭红色。颈上部饰多道弦纹，下部贴塑折枝花卉纹，肩与上腹贴饰缠枝花卉纹，胫部承托以莲瓣纹。

此尊器形高大，胎体厚重，采用刻划、贴花等装饰手法，充分表现了元代龙泉窑高超的制瓷工艺水平。

1485　元　**青釉印花花卉纹罐标本**

Yuan dynasty

Specimens of green glaze jar with stamped floral design

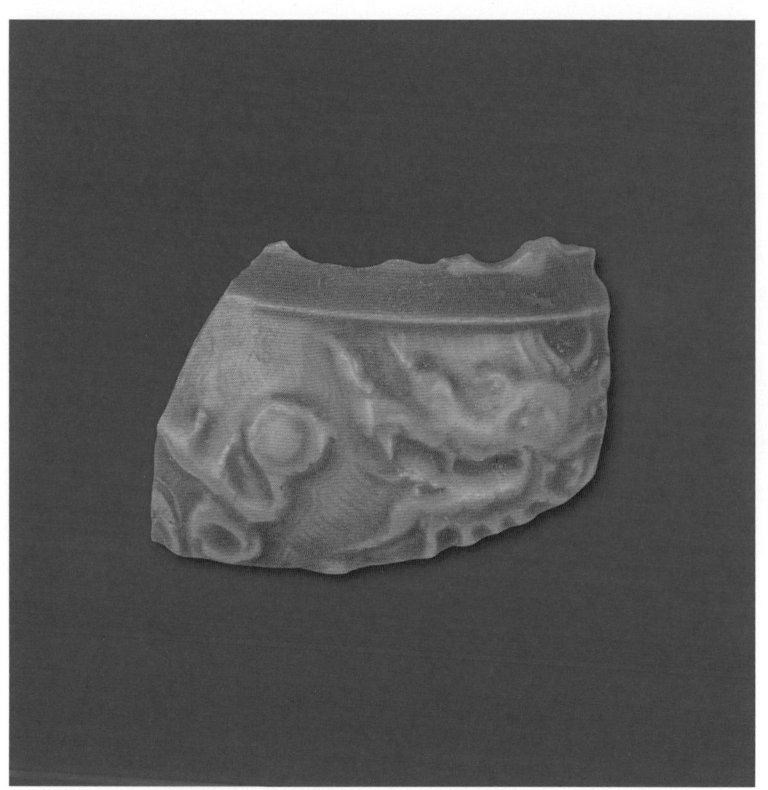

1486 **元　青釉印花龙纹罐标本**
Yuan dynasty
Specimen of green glaze jar with stamped dragon design

1487 **元　青釉印花卷枝纹炉标本**
Yuan dynasty
Specimen of green glaze burner with stamped design of branch scrolls

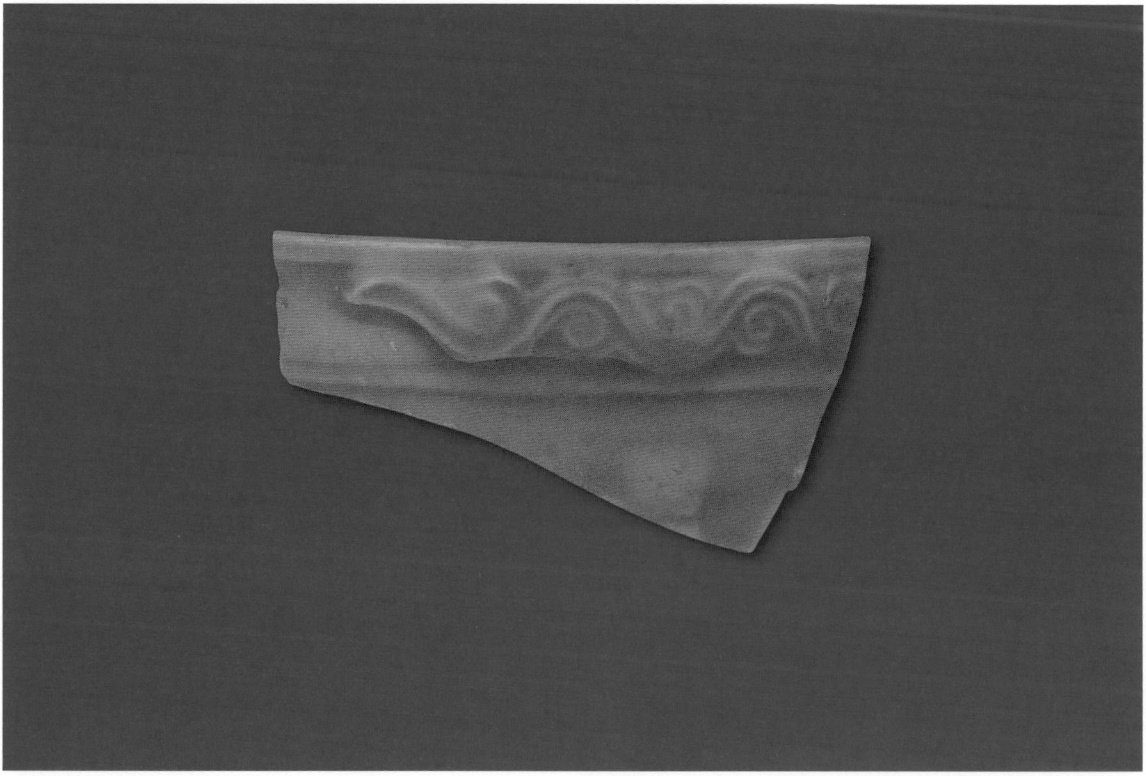

1488　元　**青釉印花八卦纹炉标本**
Yuan dynasty
Specimen of green glaze burner with stamped design of eight divinatory trigrams

1489　元　**青釉印花三足炉标本**
Yuan dynasty
Specimen of green glaze burner with three legs and stamped design

1490　元　**青釉印花八卦纹三足炉标本**

Yuan dynasty

Specimen of green glaze burner with three legs and stamped design of eight divinatory trigrams

附图

**明**

**青釉印刻花八卦纹三足筒式炉**

高 29 厘米　口径 32.6 厘米
底径 20.5 厘米
故宫博物院藏

Illustration
Ming dynasty
Green glaze barrel-shaped burner with three legs and incised design of eight divinatory trigrams

Height 29cm, mouth diameter 32.6cm, bottom diameter 20.5cm
Collected by the Palace Museum

炉直口，内折沿，筒状器身，三蹄足。灰白色胎，施青釉，釉面光亮。底部中心无釉，开一圆孔，有垫烧痕迹。腹部中间饰凸起八卦纹一周，上下各分布两道凸弦纹，弦纹间刻划缠枝花卉纹。

筒式炉又称“奁式炉”或“樽式炉”，造型仿汉代的妆奁或酒樽，为焚香用具。陶瓷筒式炉出现于宋代，定窑、汝窑、龙泉窑等著名瓷窑均有烧造，元、明时期继续流行。

1491　元

**青釉印花条纹三足炉标本**

Yuan dynasty

Specimen of green glaze burner with three legs and stamped design of strings

1492　元　**青釉印花花卉纹碗标本**

Yuan dynasty

Specimen of green glaze bowl with stamped floral design

1493　元　**青釉印花花卉纹碗标本**
Yuan dynasty
Specimen of green glaze bowl with stamped floral design

1494　元　**青釉印花莲花纹碗标本**
Yuan dynasty
Specimen of green glaze bowl with stamped lotus design

1495　元　**青釉印花莲花纹碗标本**

Yuan dynasty

Specimen of green glaze bowl with stamped lotus design

1496　元　**青釉印花双鱼纹碗标本**

Yuan dynasty

Specimen of green glaze bowl with stamped pair fish design

1497 **元 青釉印花双鱼纹碗标本**

Yuan dynasty

Specimen of green glaze bowl with stamped pair fish design

1498 **元 青釉印花双鱼纹碗标本**

Yuan dynasty

Specimen of green glaze bowl with stamped pair fish design

1499　元

**青釉印花"王"字碗标本**

Yuan dynasty

Specimen of green glaze bowl with inscription of Chinese character Wang

1500　元

**青釉印花花卉纹"清河"铭碗标本**

Yuan dynasty

Specimens of green glaze bowl with stamped floral design and inscription of Chinese characters Qing He

1501　元

**青釉印花花卉纹“清河”铭碗标本**

Yuan dynasty

Specimen of green glaze bowl with stamped floral design and inscription of Chinese characters Qing He

1502　元　**青釉印花花卉纹“金玉满堂”铭碗标本**

Yuan dynasty

Specimen of green glaze bowl with stamped floral design and inscription of Chinese characters Jin Yu Man Tang

1503 元

**青釉印花花卉纹“刘宅”铭碗标本**

Yuan dynasty

Specimen of green glaze bowl with stamped floral design and inscription of Chinese characters Liu Zhai

1504 元

**青釉印花莲花纹花口碗标本**

Yuan dynasty

Specimen of green glaze bowl with stamped lotus design and flower rim

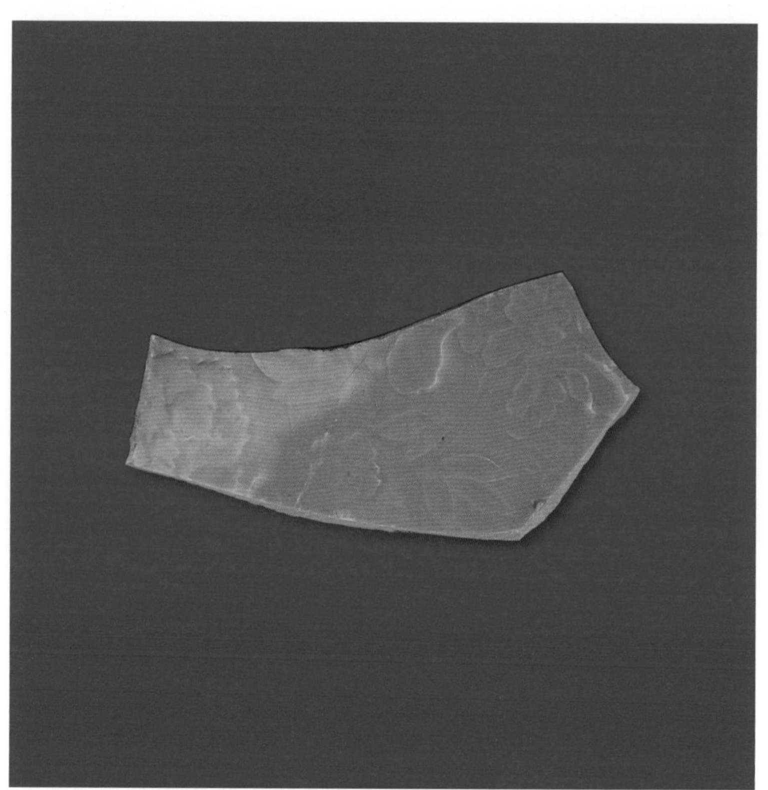

1505　元　**青釉印花花卉纹盘标本**
Yuan dynasty
Specimen of green glaze plate with stamped floral design

1506　元　**青釉印花菊花纹盘标本**
Yuan dynasty
Specimens of green glaze plate with stamped chrysanthemum design

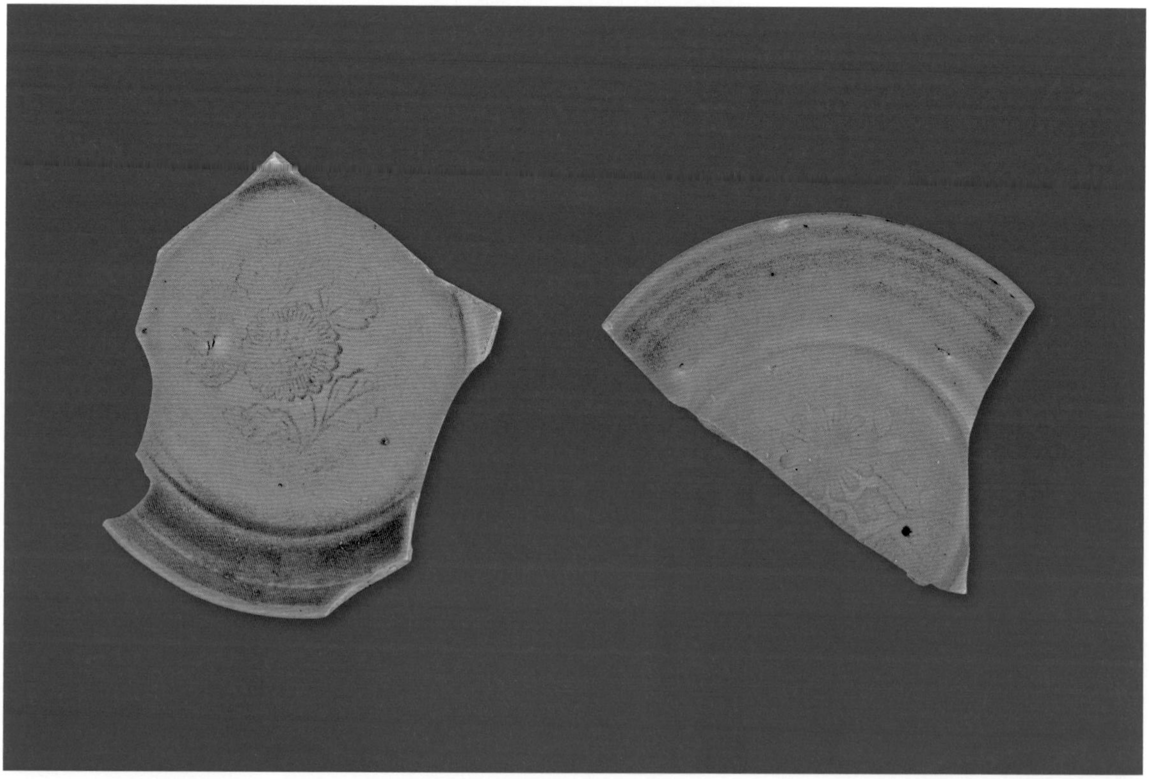

1507 元 青釉印花龙纹盘标本
Yuan dynasty Specimens of green glaze plate with stamped dragon design

1508 元 青釉印花龙纹盘标本
Yuan dynasty Specimens of green glaze plate with stamped dragon design

1509　元　**青釉印花花卉纹菱花口折沿盘标本**

Yuan dynasty　Specimen of green glaze plate with everted flange and rim in shape of water chestnut and stamped floral design

1510　元

**青釉印花龙纹菱花口折沿盘标本**

Yuan dynasty

Specimen of green glaze plate with everted flange and rim in shape of water chestnut and stamped dragon design

1511 元 **青釉印花菊瓣纹高足杯标本**

Yuan dynasty Specimen of green glaze cup with high stem and stamped chrysanthemum-petal design

1512 元 **青釉印花龙纹高足杯标本**

Yuan dynasty Specimen of green glaze cup with high stem and stamped dragon design

1513　元　**青釉里印花外刻花花卉纹碗标本**

Yuan dynasty

Specimen of green glaze bowl with stamped design inside and incised floral design outside

1514　元　**青釉里印花外刻花花卉纹碗标本**

Yuan dynasty

Specimen of green glaze bowl with stamped design inside and incised floral design outside

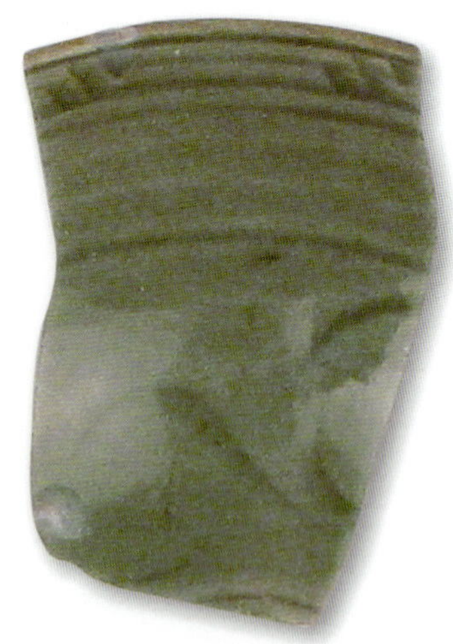

1515　元　青釉里印花花卉纹外刻花菊瓣纹碗标本
Yuan dynasty
Specimen of green glaze bowl with stamped floral design inside and incised chrysanthemum-petal design outside

1516　元　青釉里印花花卉纹外刻花莲瓣纹碗标本
Yuan dynasty
Specimen of green glaze bowl with stamped floral design inside and incised lotus-petal design outside

1517　元　**青釉里印花花卉纹外刻花莲瓣纹碗标本**
Yuan dynasty
Specimen of green glaze bowl with stamped floral design inside and incised lotus-petal design outside

1518　元　**青釉里印花花卉纹外刻花莲瓣纹碗标本**
Yuan dynasty
Specimen of green glaze bowl with stamped floral design inside and incised lotus-petal design outside

1519　元　**青釉里印花凤纹外刻花莲瓣纹碗标本**

Yuan dynasty

Specimen of green glaze bowl with stamped phoenix design inside and incised lotus-petal design outside

1520　元　**青釉里印花花卉纹“和高”铭外刻花碗标本**

Yuan dynasty

Specimen of green glaze bowl with stamped floral design and inscription of Chinese characters He Gao inside and incised design outside

1521 元 青釉里印花花卉纹外刻弦纹花口碗标本

Yuan dynasty

Specimen of green glaze bowl with flower rim and stamped floral design inside and incised strings outside

1522 元 青釉里印花菊瓣纹外刻花菊瓣纹花口碗标本

Yuan dynasty

Specimen of green glaze bowl with flower rim and stamped chrysanthemum-petal design inside and incised chrysanthemum-petal design outside

1523　元　青釉里刻花外印花花卉纹碗标本
Yuan dynasty
Specimen of green glaze bowl with incised design inside and stamped floral design outside

1524　元　青釉里印划花花卉纹外刻花莲瓣纹碗标本
Yuan dynasty
Specimen of green glaze bowl with stamped floral design inside and incised lotus-petal design outside

1525　元　**青釉刻花条纹盖罐标本**

Yuan dynasty

Specimens of green glaze jar with cover and incised design of strings

附图

**元　青釉刻花条纹荷叶式盖罐**

高 11.3 厘米　口径 9.7 厘米
足径 6.9 厘米
故宫博物院藏

Illustration
Yuan dynasty　Green glaze jar with cover in shape of lotus leaf and incised design of strings

Height 11.3cm, mouth diameter 9.7cm, foot diameter 6.9cm
Collected by the Palace Museum

罐圆唇，敛口，深腹，下腹圆收，圈足。灰白胎，细密坚致。白釉泛灰，光润，施釉近底足。

1526　元　**青釉刻花花卉纹碗标本**

Yuan dynasty　Specimen of green glaze bowl with incised floral design

1527　元　**青釉里刻花荷莲纹外刻花莲瓣纹碗标本**

Yuan dynasty　Specimen of green glaze bowl with incised lotus design inside and incised lotus-petal design outside

1528　元　**青釉刻花菊花纹盘标本**
Yuan dynasty
Specimen of green glaze plate with incised chrysanthemum design

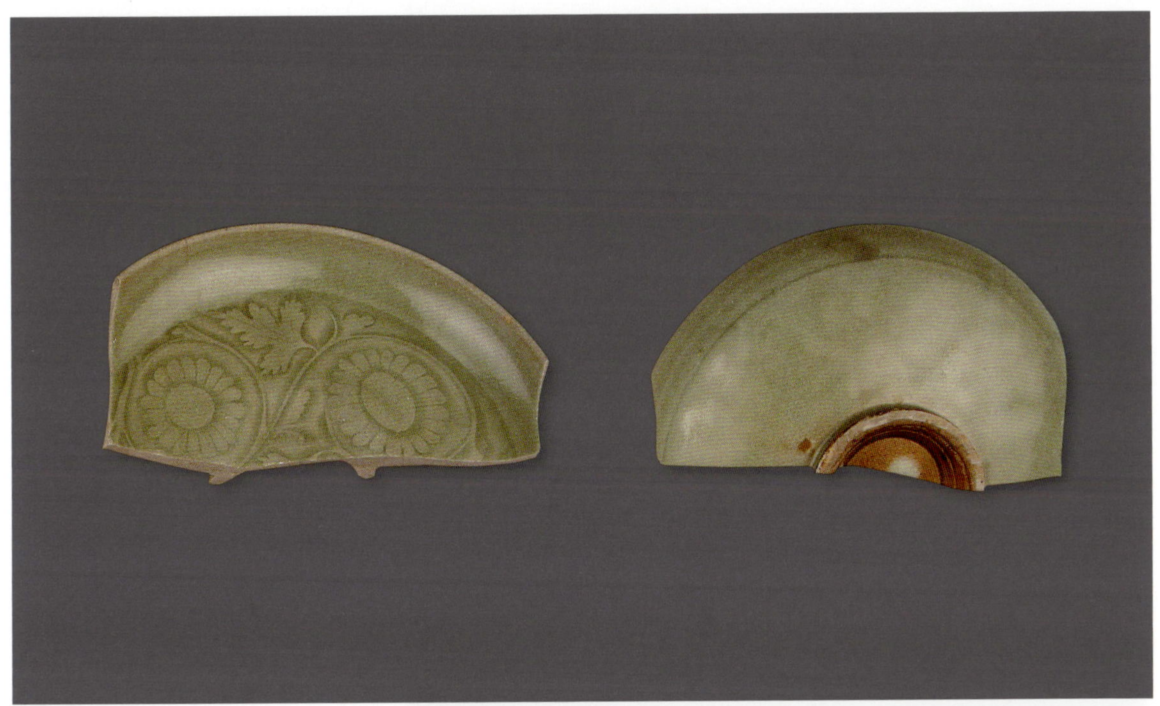

1529　元　**青釉刻花几何纹盘标本**
Yuan dynasty
Specimen of green glaze plate with incised design of geometric patterns

1530 元

**青釉刻花花卉纹折沿盘标本**

Yuan dynasty

Specimen of green glaze plate with everted flange and incised floral design

1531 元

**青釉刻花花卉纹花口花盆标本**

Yuan dynasty

Specimens of green glaze flower pot with incised floral design and flower rim

1532 元

**青釉刻划印花花卉纹盘标本**

Yuan dynasty

Specimen of green glaze plate with incised and stamped floral design

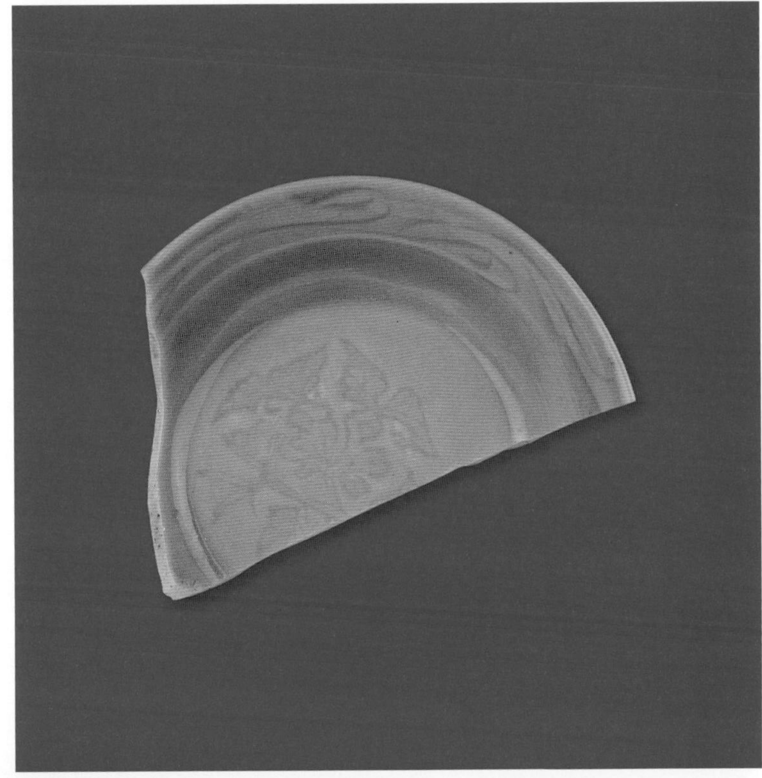

1533 元

**青釉刻划花莲花纹高足杯标本**

Yuan dynasty

Specimen of green glaze cup with high stem and incised lotus design

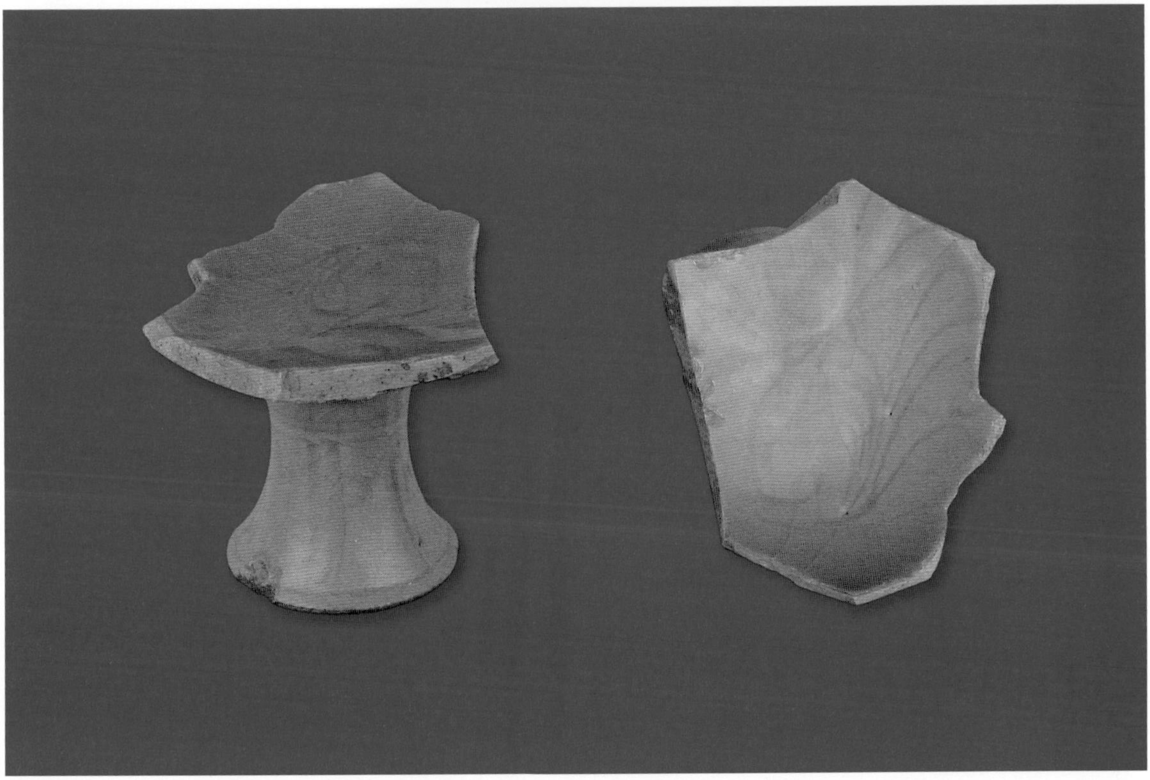

1534　元　青釉划花花卉纹印字菱花口折沿盘标本
Yuan dynasty
Specimen of green glaze plate with everted flange and rim in shape of water chestnut and incised floral design

1535　元　青釉划花凤纹菱花口折沿盘标本
Yuan dynasty
Specimen of green glaze plate with everted flange and rim in shape of water chestnut and incised phoenix design

1536　元　青釉贴花鼓钉纹炉标本
Yuan dynasty
Specimen of green glaze burner with drum-nail and applied design

1537　元
青釉露胎贴花人物纹托盘标本
Yuan dynasty
Specimen of green glaze saucer with design of unglazed figures

1538　元　青釉褐斑八方盘标本

Yuan dynasty

Specimen of green glaze octagonal plate with brown splashes

附图

**元　青釉褐斑八方盘**

高 3 厘米　口径 16.5 厘米
足径 4.7 厘米
故宫博物院藏

Illustration
Yuan dynasty
Green glaze octagonal plate with brown splashes

Height 3cm, mouth diameter 16.5cm,
foot diameter 4.7cm
Collected by the Palace Museum

盘呈八方形，折沿，浅斜腹，圈足。造型规整，棱角分明。灰白色胎。通体施青釉，釉面装饰褐彩斑点。圈足底边无釉，呈浅赭红色。

以褐斑作装饰，至迟在西晋青瓷上已普遍出现。元代龙泉窑继承和发展了这一技法，利用含铁量较高的材料，在青釉瓷器上点染，烧成后即呈褐斑装饰。

1539　元　青釉红斑碗（匜）标本
Yuan dynasty
Specimen of green glaze bowl (ewer) with red splashes

1540　明
青釉刻花花卉纹高足碗标本
Ming dynasty
Specimen of green glaze bowl with high stem and incised floral design

1541 元 窑具标本
Yuan dynasty
Specimens of kiln furniture

1542 元 窑具标本
Yuan dynasty
Specimen of kiln furniture

1543 元 窑具标本
Yuan dynasty
Specimen of kiln furniture

龙泉（杉树连山）窑遗址
Ruin of Longquan kiln
at Shanshulianshan

龙泉（杉树连山）窑遗址
Ruin of Longquan kiln
at Shanshulianshan

1544 **南宋至元 青釉瓶标本**
From Southern Song dynasty to Yuan dynasty
Specimen of green glaze vase

1545 **南宋至元 青釉罐标本**
From Southern Song dynasty to Yuan dynasty
Specimens of green glaze jar

1546 **南宋至元　青釉盘标本**

From Southern Song dynasty to Yuan dynasty

Specimens of green glaze plate

1547　**南宋至元　青釉折沿盘标本**
From Southern Song dynasty to Yuan dynasty
Specimen of green glaze plate with everted flange

1548　**南宋至元　青釉折沿盘标本**
From Southern Song dynasty to Yuan dynasty
Specimens of green glaze plate with everted flange

1549 **南宋至元 青釉印花碗标本**

From Southern Song dynasty to Yuan dynasty

Specimen of green glaze bowl with stamped design

1550 **南宋至元 青釉模印菊瓣纹折沿盘标本**

From Southern Song dynasty to Yuan dynasty

Specimen of green glaze plate with everted flange and molded design of chrysanthemum-petals

1551　南宋至元　青釉模印菊瓣纹折沿盘标本
From Southern Song dynasty to Yuan dynasty
Specimens of green glaze plate with everted flange and molded design of chrysanthemum-petals

1552 **南宋至元　青釉印花双鱼洗标本**

From Southern Song dynasty to Yuan dynasty

Specimen of green glaze washer with stamped design of pair fish

1553 南宋至元 青釉刻花花卉纹盘标本
From Southern Song dynasty to Yuan dynasty
Specimen of green glaze plate with incised floral design

1554 南宋至元 青釉刻花菊瓣纹盘标本
From Southern Song dynasty to Yuan dynasty
Specimen of green glaze plate with incised chrysanthemum-petal design

1555 **南宋至元 青釉里划花篦划纹外弦纹碗标本**
From Southern Song dynasty to Yuan dynasty
Specimen of green glaze bowl with comb-incised design inside and incised string design outside

1556 **南宋至元 青釉里划花篦点纹外刻线纹碗标本**
From Southern Song dynasty to Yuan dynasty
Specimen of green glaze bowl with comb-incised dot design inside and incised line design outside

1557 **南宋至元　窑具标本**

From Southern Song dynasty to Yuan dynasty

Specimens of kiln furniture

**龙泉（枫树坪官厂）窑遗址**
Ruin of Longquan kiln at Fengshupingguanchang

**龙泉（枫树坪官厂）窑遗址**
Ruin of Longquan kiln at Fengshupingguanchang

1558 **元 青釉罐标本**
Yuan dynasty
Specimen of green glaze jar

1559 **元 青釉炉标本**
Yuan dynasty
Specimens of green glaze burner

1560 **元　青釉碗标本**
Yuan dynasty
Specimen of green glaze bowl

1561 **元　青釉高足碗标本**
Yuan dynasty
Specimen of green glaze bowl with high stem

1562 元 青釉盘标本

Yuan dynasty

Specimens of green glaze plate

1563 元 青釉折沿盘标本
Yuan dynasty
Specimen of green glaze plate with everted flange

1564 元 青釉弦纹炉标本
Yuan dynasty
Specimen of green glaze burner with design of strings

1565 元 青釉印花八卦炉标本
Yuan dynasty Specimen of green glaze burner with design of eight divinatory trigrams

1566 元 青釉印花鼓钉八卦纹炉标本

Yuan dynasty Specimens of green glaze burner with design of drum nails and eight divinatory trigrams

1567 元 青釉印花花卉纹碗标本

Yuan dynasty Specimen of green glaze bowl with stamped flower design

## 1568　元　青釉印花花卉纹盘标本

Yuan dynasty

Specimens of green glaze plate with stamped floral design

1569 元 **青釉模印菊瓣纹折沿盘标本**

Yuan dynasty

Specimen of green glaze plate with everted flange and molded design of chrysanthemum-petals

1570 元 **青釉模印菊瓣纹折沿花口盘标本**

Yuan dynasty

Specimens of green glaze plate with everted flange and flower rim and molded design of chrysanthemum-petals

1571　**元　青釉刻花罐标本**
Yuan dynasty
Specimen of green glaze jar with incised design

1572　**元至明**
**青釉刻花花卉纹碗标本**
From Yuan dynasty to Ming dynasty
Specimen of green glaze bowl with incised flower design

1573 **元至明**

**青釉刻花花卉纹盘标本**

From Yuan dynasty to Ming dynasty
Specimen of green glaze plate with incised floral design

1574 **元至明**

**青釉刻花花卉纹高足杯标本**

From Yuan dynasty to Ming dynasty
Specimen of green glaze cup with high stem and incised floral design

**龙泉（安仁）窑遗址瓷片遗存**

Pileup of porcelain parts at the ruin of Longquan kiln at Anren

1575　元　青釉印"金玉满堂"铭碗标本
Yuan dynasty　Specimen of green glaze bowl with inscription of Chinese characters Jin Yu Man Tang

1576　元　青釉印花花卉纹碗标本
Yuan dynasty　Specimen of green glaze bowl with stamped floral design

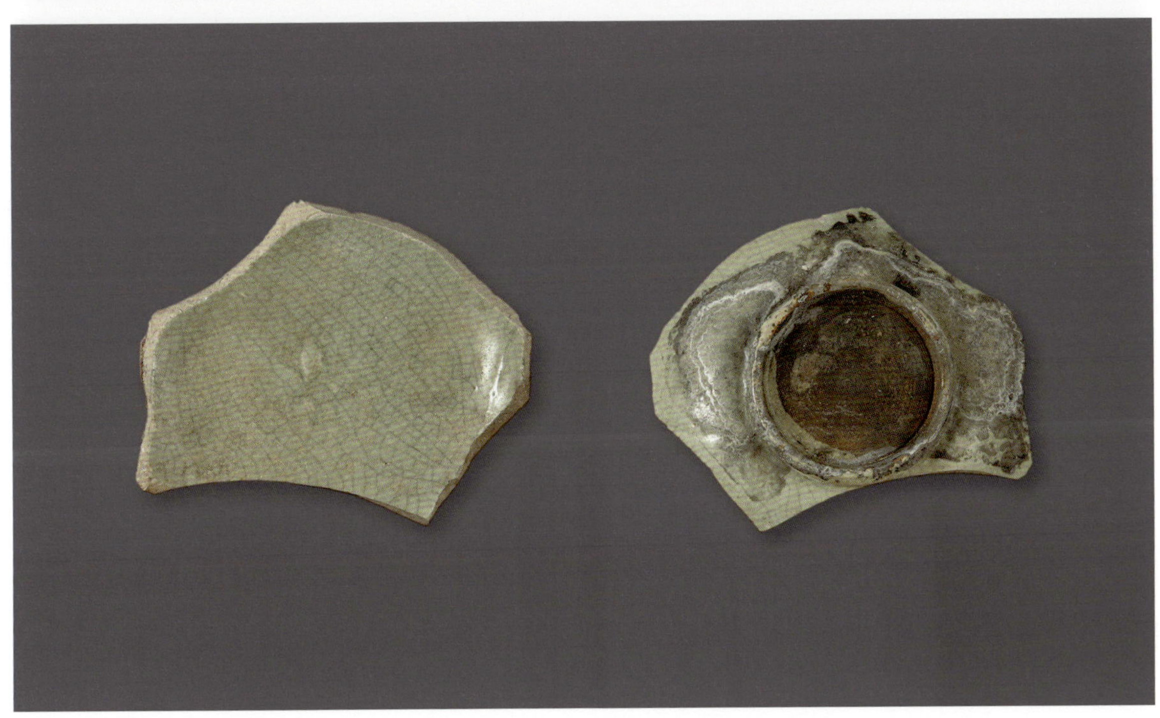

1577　**元　青釉印花花卉纹碗标本**

Yuan dynasty

Specimens of green glaze bowl with stamped floral design

1578　元　青釉印花花卉纹碗标本

Yuan dynasty

Specimen of green glaze bowl with stamped floral design

## 1579 元 青釉印花花卉纹碗标本

Yuan dynasty

Specimens of green glaze bowl with stamped floral design

1580　**元　青釉印花菊瓣纹碗标本**

Yuan dynasty　Specimen of green glaze bowl with stamped chrysanthemum-petal design

1581　**元　青釉印花花卉纹花口碗标本**

Yuan dynasty　Specimen of green glaze bowl with stamped floral design and flower rim

1582 **元 青釉印花花卉纹盘标本**

Yuan dynasty

Specimens of green glaze plate with stamped floral design

1583 **元 青釉印花花卉纹盘标本**

Yuan dynasty

Specimens of green glaze plate with stamped floral design

1584　元　青釉印花花卉纹盘标本
Yuan dynasty
Specimen of green glaze plate with stamped floral design

1585　元　青釉印花花卉纹花式盘标本
Yuan dynasty
Specimen of green glaze flower-shaped plate with stamped floral design

1586　元　**青釉模印菊瓣纹盘标本**

Yuan dynasty

Specimens of green glaze plate with molded design of chrysanthemum-petals

1587　**元　青釉模印菊瓣纹折沿花口盘标本**

Yuan dynasty

Specimens of green glaze plate with flower rim and everted flange and molded design of chrysanthemum-petals

1588 元 青釉印花鹿纹高足杯标本

Yuan dynasty Specimen of green glaze cup with high stem and stamped deer design

1589 元 青釉印花“仲夫”铭高足杯标本

Yuan dynasty Specimen of green glaze cup with high stem and inscription of Chinese characters Zhong Fu

1590 元 青釉里印花花卉纹外刻线纹碗标本

Yuan dynasty

Specimens of green glaze bowl with stamped floral design inside and incised line design outside

1591　元　**青釉里印花菊瓣纹外刻花莲瓣纹碗标本**

Yuan dynasty

Specimen of green glaze bowl with stamped chrysanthemum-petal design inside and incised lotus-petal design outside

1592　元　**青釉刻花莲瓣纹碗标本**

Yuan dynasty

Specimen of green glaze bowl with incised lotus-petal design

1593 元 **青釉刻花莲瓣纹碗标本**

Yuan dynasty

Specimen of green glaze bowl with incised lotus-petal design

1594 元 **青釉刻花折沿盘标本**

Yuan dynasty

Specimen of green glaze plate with everted flange and incised design

1595 元 青釉刻花高足杯标本

Yuan dynasty

Specimens of green glaze cup with high stem and incised design

1596 元 青釉里印刻划花花卉纹外刻花莲瓣纹碗标本

Yuan dynasty

Specimens of green glaze bowl with stamped and incised floral design inside and incised lotus-petal design outside

1597　元　青釉里印刻划花花卉纹外刻花莲瓣纹碗标本

Yuan dynasty

Specimen of green glaze bowl with stamped and incised floral design inside and incised lotus-petal design outside

1598　元　青釉里印刻划花花卉纹外刻花莲瓣纹碗标本

Yuan dynasty

Specimen of green glaze bowl with stamped and incised floral design inside and incised lotus-petal design outside

1599　元　青釉里刻划花花卉纹外刻花莲瓣纹碗标本

Yuan dynasty

Specimen of green glaze bowl with incised flower design inside and incised lotus-petal design outside

1600　元　青釉里刻划花花卉纹外刻花莲瓣纹碗标本

Yuan dynasty

Specimen of green glaze bowl with incised flower design inside and incised lotus-petal design outside

1601　元　青釉里刻划花花卉纹外刻花莲瓣纹碗标本

Yuan dynasty

Specimens of green glaze bowl with incised flower design inside and incised lotus-petal design outside

1602　元　窑具标本
Yuan dynasty
Specimen of kiln furniture

1603　元　窑具标本
Yuan dynasty
Specimens of kiln furniture

# 庆元窑

庆元窑烧瓷时间从唐代到清代，2009 年故宫博物院部分专家学者调查了该窑的黄坛、潘里垄、新窑、竹口窑。

黄坛窑。唐代瓷窑。有少量青釉盘口壶、平底碗、罐等碎片堆积。青釉色深，有的碗里心有较大的支烧痕。

潘里垄窑。宋代至元代瓷窑，分 Y1、Y2 两处，Y1 依坡而建，似有窑迹存在。主要烧造黑釉碗。胎色黑，与福建北部部分瓷窑相似。造型有敞口、敛口、出棱几种。釉色有黑、酱等。有的黑亮，有的出现兔毫纹。修足比较规矩，比福建的略细。垫饼有大、小，规整、随意几种。匣钵有筒形、“M”形。匣钵小而深，适合烧造盏类器物。

新窑。包括新窑 1、新窑 2，唐至明代瓷窑，位于竹口镇新窑村，瓯江从乡间流过。烧造龙泉窑系产品，有碗、折沿花口盘。碗足小，底心有釉，装饰简单的刻划花。垫饼支烧。

竹口窑。元代至明代瓷窑。采集标本有碗，有“福”、“清”字，阴文印花装饰，外多刻线纹。还有盘、罐、盖、炉、灯、卧足杯等，特别是炉的造型非常丰富，有筒式三足、扁腹三足、饼足三足、乳丁刻花三兽足及八卦炉等。

# Qingyuan Kiln

Qingyuan kiln started to fire in Tang dynasty and ended in Qing dynasty. Experts from the Palace Museum investigated kiln sites at Huangtan, Panlilong, XinyaoI, XinyaoII, Zhukouyao in 2009.

Kiln Huangtan is a Tang dynasty porcelain kiln. There are a few green glaze pots with dish-shaped mouth, bowls with flat bottom, jars and so on in the accumulation. The color of the green glaze is dark. There are relatively large spur marks inside the center of some of the bowls.

Kiln Panlilong, dated back to Song dynasty to Yuan dynasty, has two sites, YI and YII. Traces at site suggest YI was built along a slope. Principal products of YI are black glaze bowls with dark body, similar to those produced by kilns in the northern part of Fujian Province. Some bowls are with flared mouth, some with contracted mouth and some with ribs. Glaze is in black or dark brown. Some bowls are with hare's fur streaks (as on Jian wares). The feet of the bowls were well-treated, slightly thinner than that of bowls made by kilns in Fujian Province. Pads vary in size and shape. Saggars are barrel or M –shaped, small but deep, suitable for firing saucers.

Kiln Xinyao, located at Xinyao Village, Zhukou Town, is a porcelain kiln of Tang dynasty to Ming dynasty. It fired wares of Longquan kiln style, such as bowls, plates with flower rim and everted flange, etc. Bowls are with small foot, glaze in the center outside, simple decoration of incised pattern and fired using a pad against the bottom.

Kiln Zhukouyao is dated back to Yuan dynasty to Ming dynasty. Specimens collected are bowls, plates, jars, covers, burners, lamps, cups with concave foot and so on. Bowls are with Chinese character, Fu or Qing, stamped patterns in negative legend and incised lines outside. Burners are particularly rich in shapes. There are three-legged burners in shape of barrel, three-legged burners with flat belly, three-legged burners with cake alike foot, three-legged burners with animal alike foot, nipples and incised patterns, burners with design of Eight Divinatory Trigrams, etc.

**庆元（黄坛）窑遗址保护碑**
Monument for protecting ruin of Qingyuan kiln at Huangtan

**庆元（黄坛）窑遗址**
Ruin of Qingyuan kiln at Huangtan

1604 **唐　青釉瓶标本**

Tang dynasty

Specimens of green glaze vase

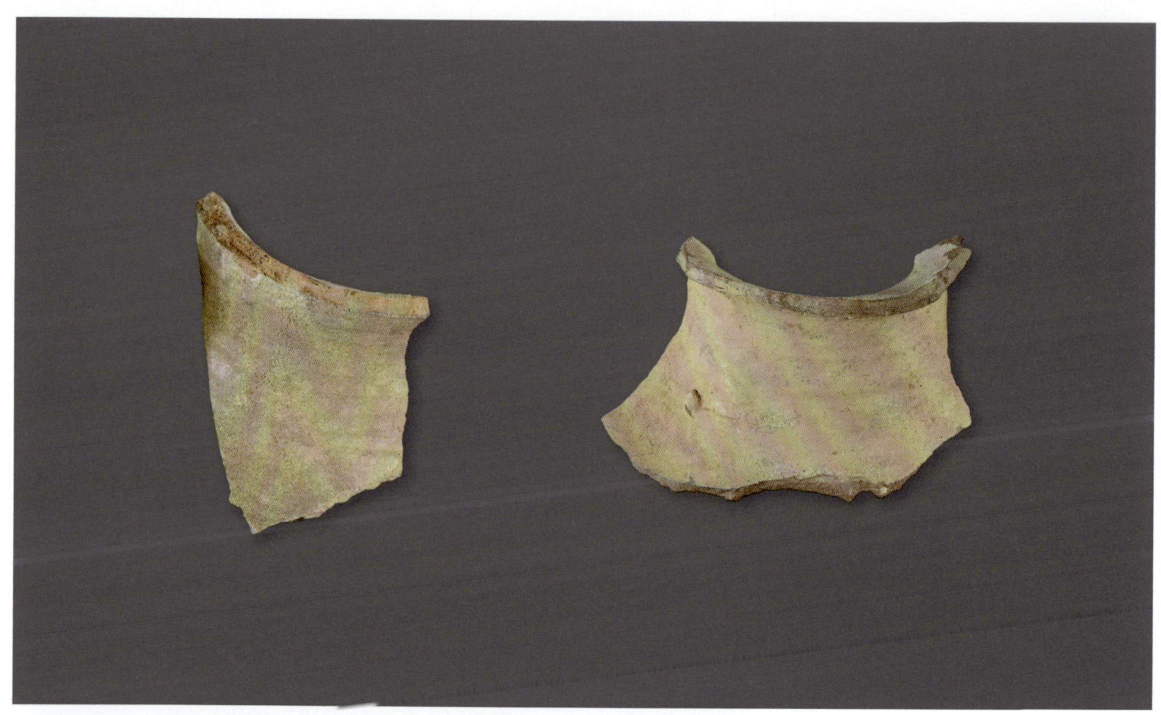

1605 **唐　青釉罐标本**

Tang dynasty

Specimen of green glaze jar

1606 **唐 青釉双系罐标本**
Tang dynasty
Specimen of green glaze jar with two handles

1607 **唐 青釉盘口壶标本**
Tang dynasty
Specimen of green glaze pot with dish-shaped mouth

1608 **唐 青釉碗标本**
Tang dynasty
Specimens of green glaze bowl

**庆元（潘里垄）窑遗址**
Ruin of Qingyuan kiln at Panlilong

**庆元（潘里垄）窑遗址瓷片遗存**
Pileup of porcelain parts at the ruin of Qingyuan kiln at Panlilong

1609　宋　黑釉碗标本

Song dynasty

Specimens of black glaze bowl

1610 **宋　黑釉碗标本**

Song dynasty

Specimens of black glaze bowl

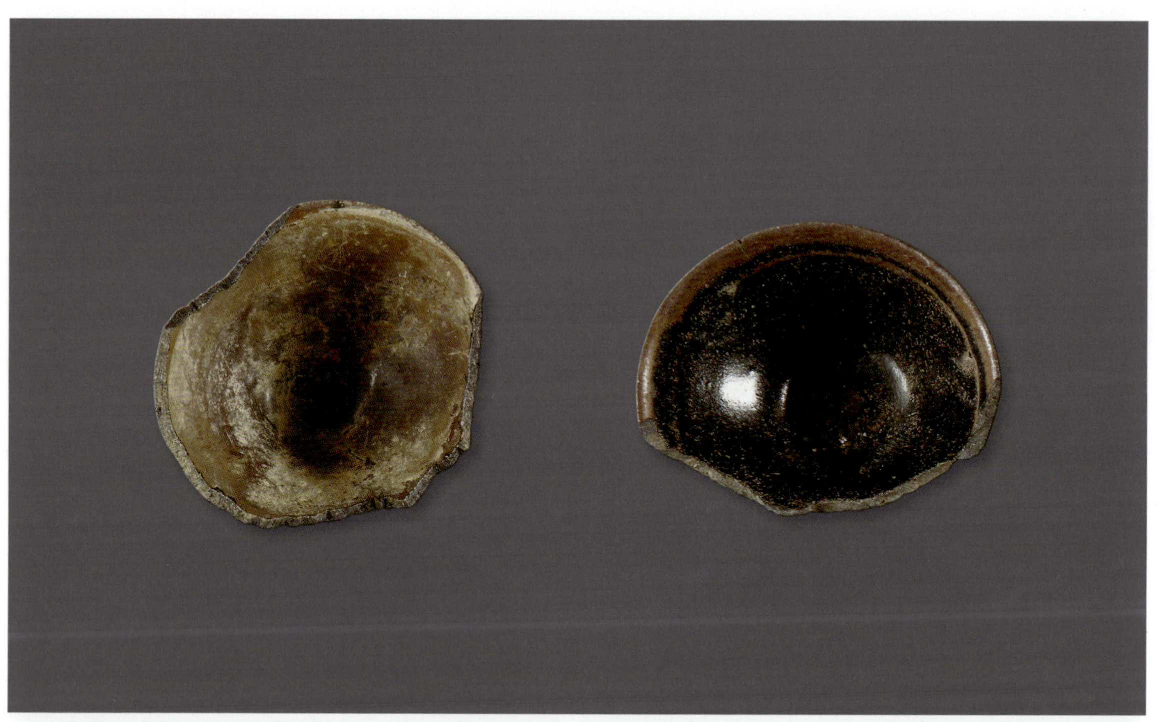

1611　**宋　黑釉碗标本**

Song dynasty

Specimens of black glaze bowl

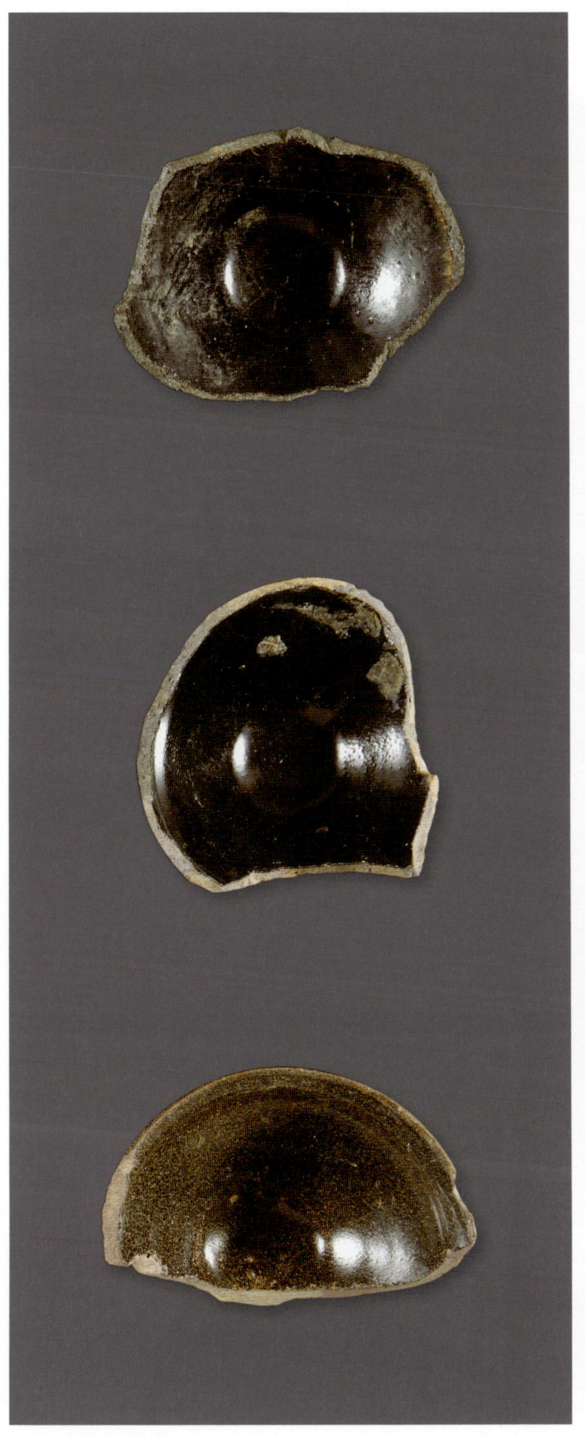

1612 **宋 黑釉碗标本**
Song dynasty
Specimens of black glaze bowl

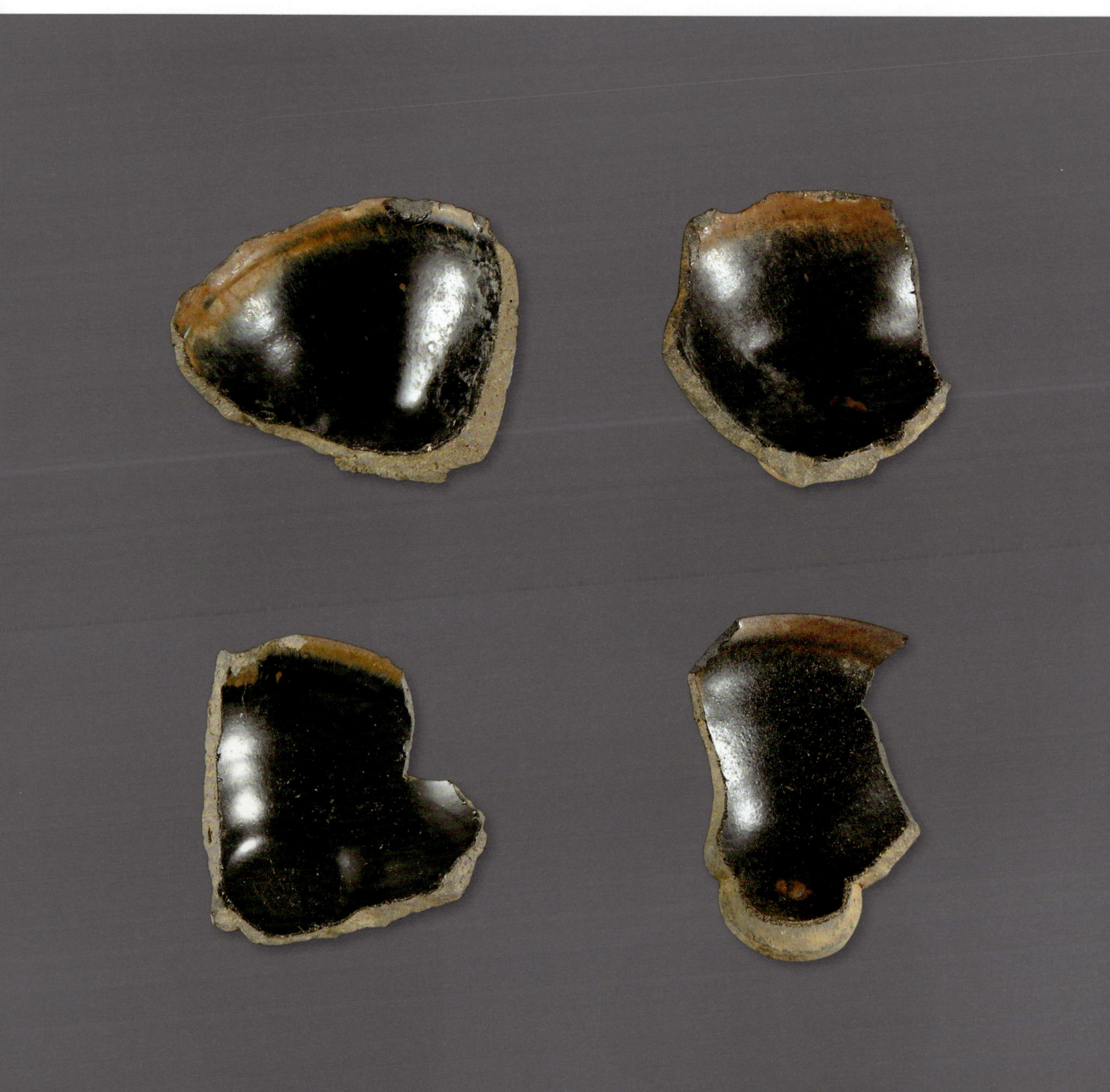

1613 **宋 黑釉碗标本**

Song dynasty

Specimens of black glaze bowl

1614 **宋　黑釉碗标本**

Song dynasty

Specimens of black glaze bowl

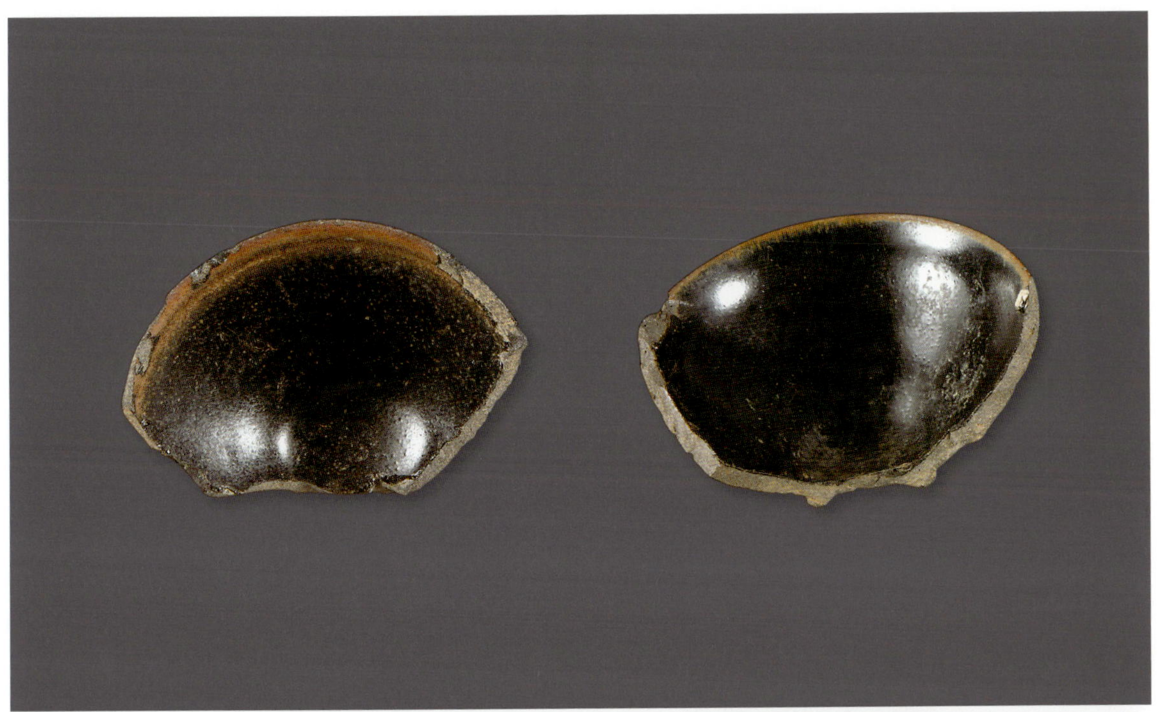

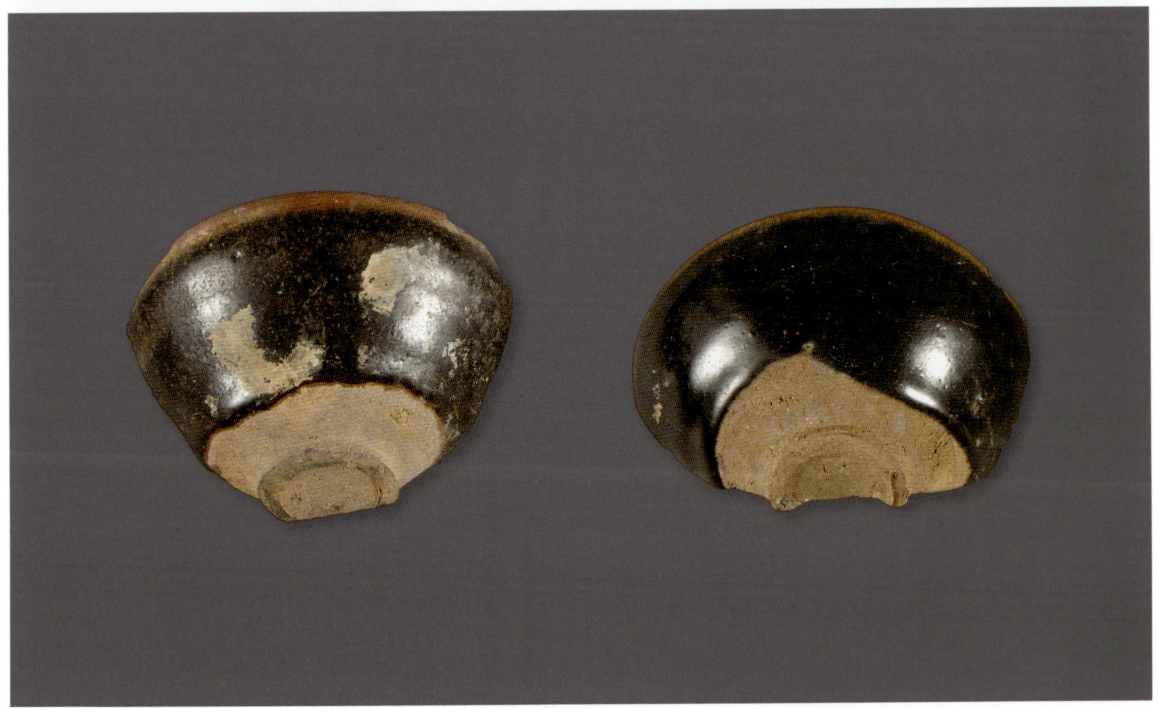

1615 **宋 黑釉碗标本**
Song dynasty
Specimens of black glaze bowl

1616　元　青釉碗标本

Yuan dynasty

Specimens of green glaze bowl

1617　元　青釉碗标本

Yuan dynasty

Specimens of green glaze bowl

1618 **宋至元 窑具标本**

From Song dynasty to Yuan dynasty

Specimens of kiln furniture

1619　宋至元　窑具标本
From Song dynasty to Yuan dynasty
Specimen of kiln furniture

庆元新窑 1 遗址
Ruin of Qingyuan kiln at Xinyao I

庆元新窑 1 遗址
Ruin of Qingyuan kiln at Xinyao I

1620 **明　青釉炉标本**
Ming dynasty
Specimen of green glaze burner

1621 **明　青釉器标本**
Ming dynasty
Specimen of green glaze ware

1622 **明　青釉碗标本**

Ming dynasty

Specimens of green glaze bowl

1623 **明　青釉碗标本**
Ming dynasty
Specimen of green glaze bowl

1624 **明　青釉碗标本**
Ming dynasty
Specimen of green glaze bowl

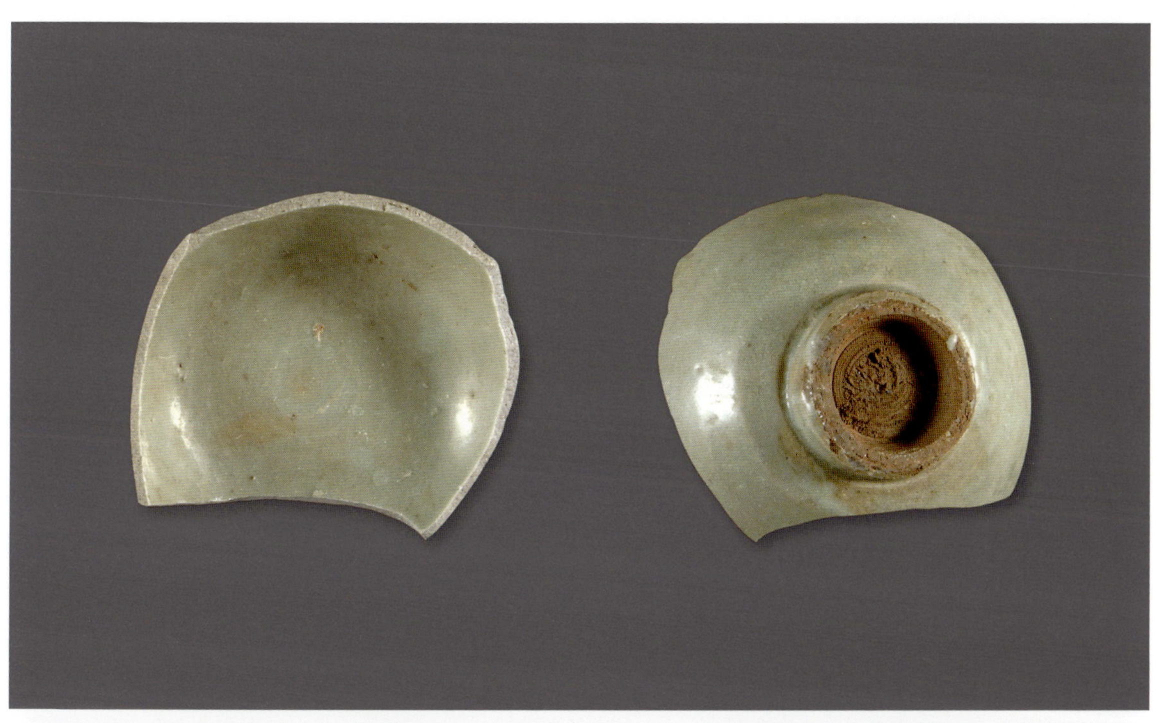

1625 **明　青釉碗标本**

Ming dynasty

Specimens of green glaze bowl

1626 **明　青釉碗标本**

Ming dynasty

Specimens of green glaze bowl

1627 **明 青釉盘标本**
Ming dynasty
Specimen of green glaze plate

1628 **明 青釉高足杯标本**
Ming dynasty
Specimen of green glaze cup with high stem

1629 **明　青釉印花双鱼纹碗标本**
Ming dynasty　Specimen of green glaze bowl with stamped design of pair fish

1630 **明　青釉刻花菊瓣纹碗标本**
Ming dynasty　Specimens of green glaze bowl with incised chrysanthemum-petal design

1631 **明　青釉里刻花花卉纹外刻线纹碗标本**
Ming dynasty　Specimen of green glaze bowl with incised floral design inside and incised line design outside

1632 **明　青釉刻花叶纹花口盘标本**
Ming dynasty　Specimen of green glaze plate with flower rim and incised leaf design

庆元新窑 2 遗址保护碑

Monument for protecting the ruin of Qingyuan kiln at Xinyao II

庆元新窑 2 遗址

Ruin of Qingyuan kiln at Xinyao II

1633　元　青釉碗标本
Yuan dynasty
Specimens of green glaze bowl

1634 **元 青釉碗标本**

Yuan dynasty

Specimens of green glaze bowl

1635 **元 青釉碗标本**
Yuan dynasty
Specimens of green glaze bowl

1636 **元　青釉碗标本**
Yuan dynasty
Specimen of green glaze bowl

1637 **元　青釉花口盘标本**
Yuan dynasty
Specimens of green glaze plate with flower rim

**庆元（竹口）窑遗址**
Ruin of Qingyuan kiln at Zhukou

**庆元（竹口）窑瓷片遗存**
Pileup of porcelain parts at the ruin of Qingyuan kiln at Zhukou

1638　**元至明　青釉瓶标本**
From Yuan dynasty to Ming dynasty
Specimen of green glaze vase

1639　**元至明　青釉梅瓶标本**
From Yuan dynasty to Ming dynasty
Specimen of green glaze prunus vase

1640　**元至明　青釉炉标本**
From Yuan dynasty to Ming dynasty
Specimen of green glaze burner

1641　**元至明　青釉三足炉标本**
From Yuan dynasty to Ming dynasty
Specimens of green glaze burner with three-legged design

1642 元至明 青釉三足炉标本
From Yuan dynasty to Ming dynasty
Specimens of green glaze burner with three-legged design

1643　**元至明　青釉三足炉标本**
From Yuan dynasty to Ming dynasty
Specimens of green glaze burner with three legs

1644　**元至明　青釉灯标本**
From Yuan dynasty to Ming dynasty
Specimen of green glaze lamp

1645 **元至明　青釉碗标本**

From Yuan dynasty to Ming dynasty

Specimens of green glaze bowl

1646 **元至明　青釉碗标本**

From Yuan dynasty to Ming dynasty

Specimens of green glaze bowl

1647 **元至明 青釉碗标本**
From Yuan dynasty to Ming dynasty
Specimen of green glaze bowl

1648 **元至明 青釉弦纹炉标本**
From Yuan dynasty to Ming dynasty
Specimens of green glaze burner with design of strings

1649 **元至明　青釉弦纹炉标本**
From Yuan dynasty to Ming dynasty
Specimen of green glaze burner with design of strings

1650 **元至明　青釉印花八卦纹三足炉标本**
From Yuan dynasty to Ming dynasty
Specimens of green glaze burner with stamped design of eight divinatory trigrams and three legs

1651　元至明　青釉印花八卦纹三足炉标本

From Yuan dynasty to Ming dynasty

Specimens of green glaze burner with stamped design of eight divinatory trigrams and three legs

1652 **元至明　青釉印花八卦纹三足炉标本**

From Yuan dynasty to Ming dynasty

Specimens of green glaze burner with stamped design of eight divinatory trigrams and three legs

1653 **元至明　青釉印花花卉纹碗标本**

From Yuan dynasty to Ming dynasty

Specimen of green glaze bowl with stamped floral design

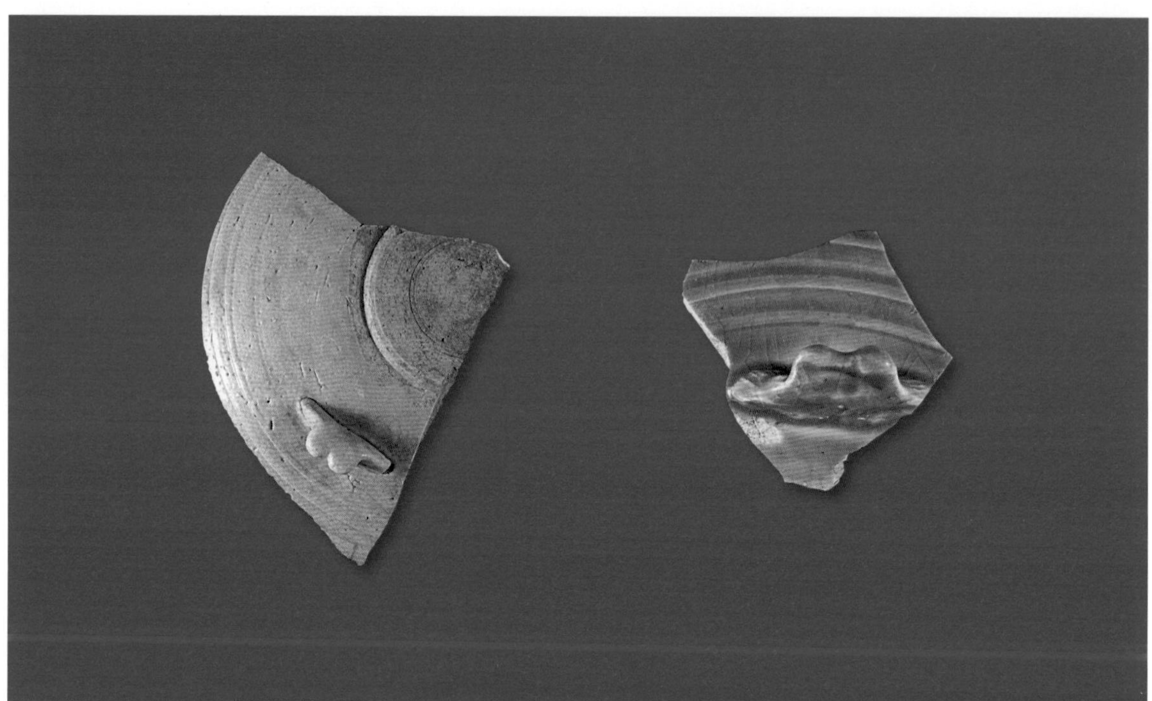

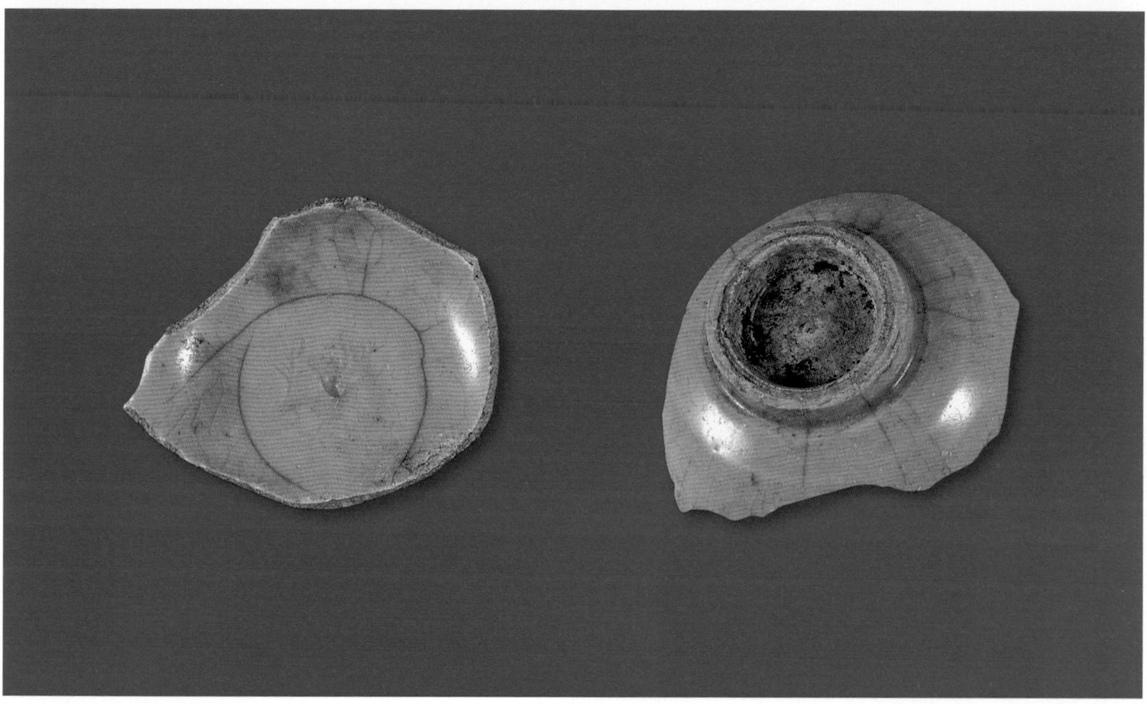

1654　元至明　青釉印花花卉纹碗标本
From Yuan dynasty to Ming dynasty
Specimens of green glaze bowl with stamped floral design

1655　元至明　青釉印花花卉纹碗标本
From Yuan dynasty to Ming dynasty
Specimens of green glaze bowl with stamped floral design

1656　**元至明**
**青釉刻花叶纹瓶标本**
From Yuan dynasty to Ming dynasty
Specimen of green glaze vase with incised leaf design

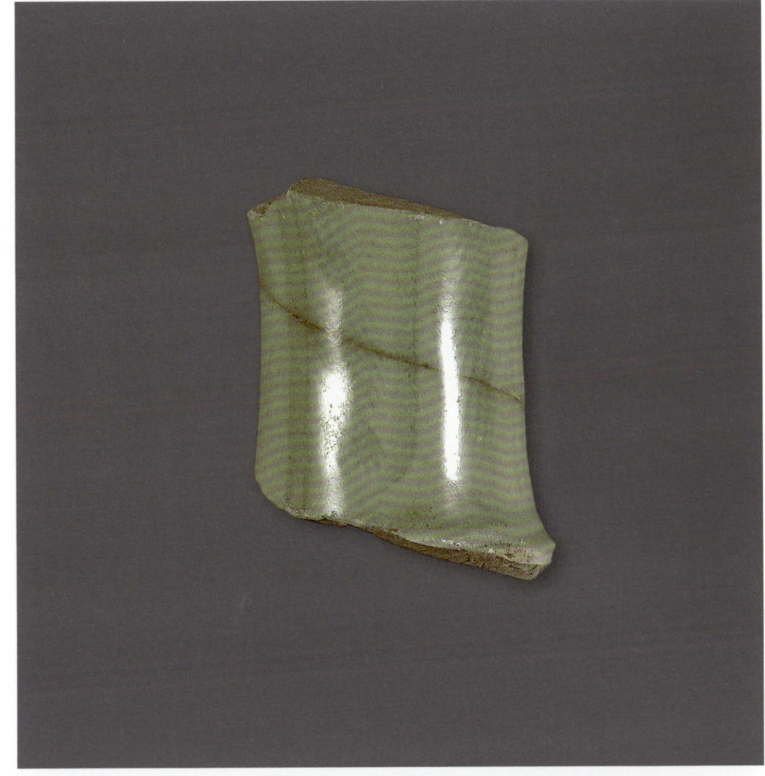

1657　**元至明**
**青釉刻弦纹瓶标本**
From Yuan dynasty to Ming dynasty
Specimen of green glaze vase with incised string design

1658 **明　青釉印花人物纹碗标本**
Ming dynasty　Specimen of green glaze bowl with stamped figure design

1659 **明　青釉印花银锭纹碗标本**
Ming dynasty　Specimen of green glaze bowl with stamped design of silver ingot

1660　**明　青釉印花"福"字碗标本**

Ming dynasty

Specimens of green glaze bowl with stamped Chinese character Fu

1661　**明　青釉印花"富"字碗标本**

Ming dynasty

Specimen of green glaze bowl with stamped Chinese character Fu

1662　**明　青釉印花"吉"字 碗标本**

Ming dynasty　Specimen of green glaze bowl with stamped Chinese character Ji

1663　明　青釉印花“玉”字碗标本
Ming dynasty　Specimen of green glaze bowl with stamped Chinese character Yu

1664　明　青釉里印花“满”字碗标本
Ming dynasty　Specimen of green glaze bowl with stamped Chinese character Man

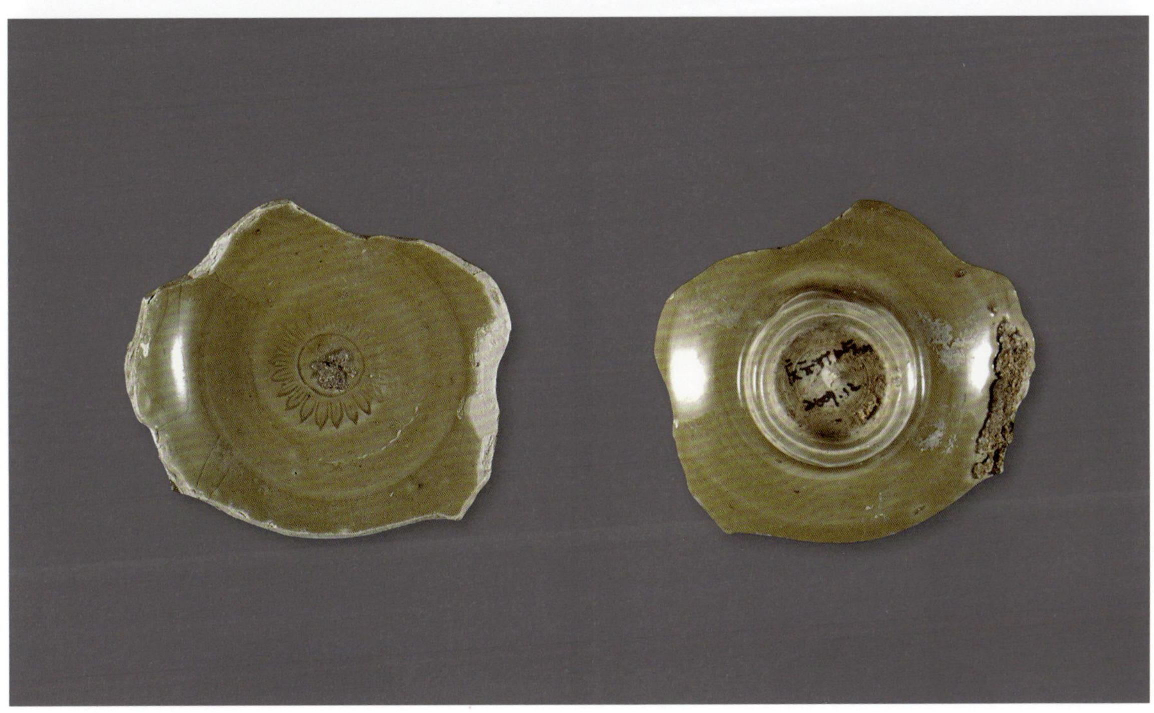

1665 **明 青釉印花"满"字碗标本**

Ming dynasty

Specimen of green glaze bowl with stamped Chinese character Man

1666 **明 青釉里印花"满"字外刻菊瓣纹碗标本**

Ming dynasty Specimen of green glaze bowl with stamped Chinese character Man inside and incised chrysanthemum-petal design outside

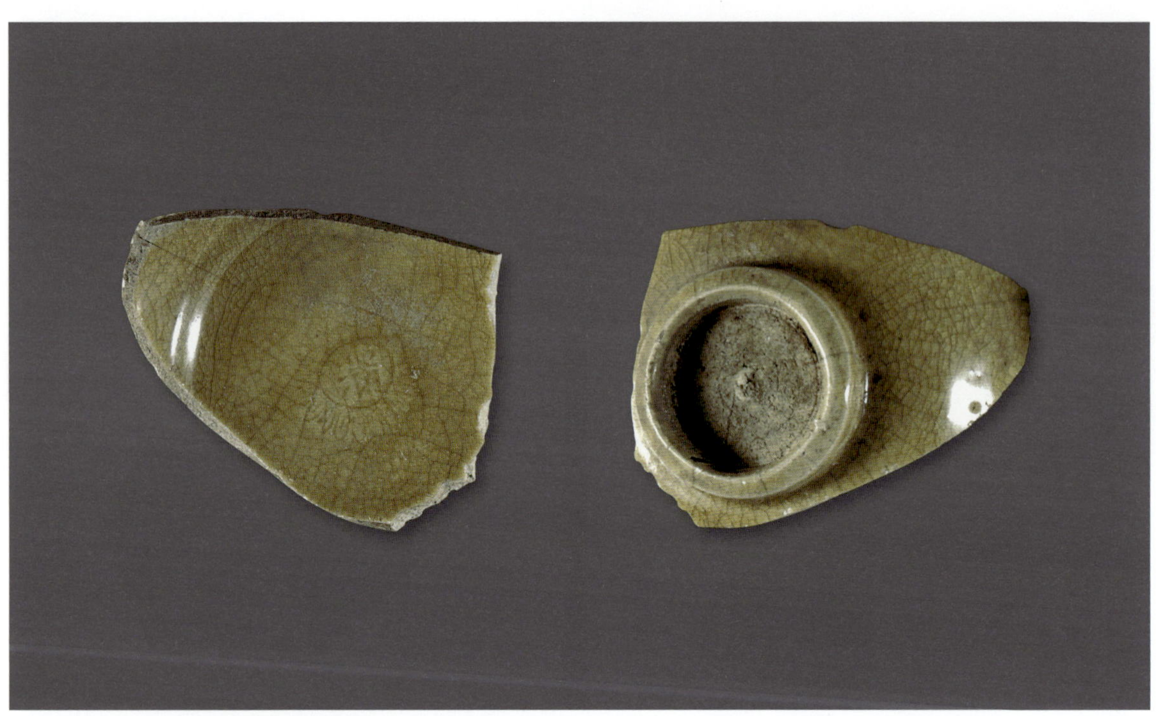

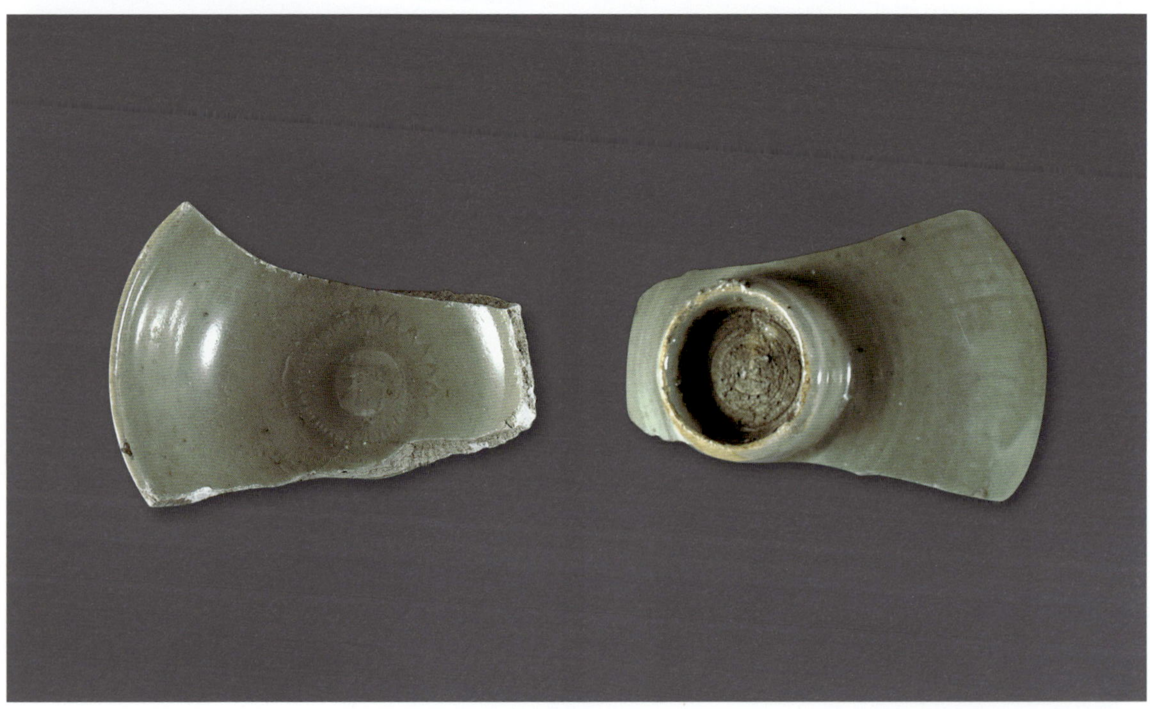

1667　**明　青釉里印花“满”字外刻菊瓣纹碗标本**

Ming dynasty

Specimens of green glaze bowl with stamped Chinese character Man inside and incised chrysanthemum-petal design outside

1668 明 青釉里印花“满”字外刻线纹碗标本
Ming dynasty
Specimen of green glaze bowl with stamped Chinese character Man inside and incised lines outside

1669 明 青釉里印花人物纹外刻菊瓣纹碗标本
Ming dynasty
Specimen of green glaze bowl with stamped figure design inside and incised chrysanthemum-petals outside

1670　明　青釉里印花银锭纹外刻花瓣纹碗标本

Ming dynasty

Specimen of green glaze bowl with stamped design of silver ingot inside and incised design of flower-petals outside

1671　明　青釉里印花“满”字外刻莲瓣纹盘标本

Ming dynasty

Specimen of green glaze plate with stamped Chinese character Man inside and incised lotus-petals outside

1672 **明 青釉刻花瓶标本**

Ming dynasty

Specimen of green glaze vase with incised design

1673 **明**

**青釉刻花花卉纹三足炉标本**

Ming dynasty

Specimen of green glaze burner with three legs and incised floral design

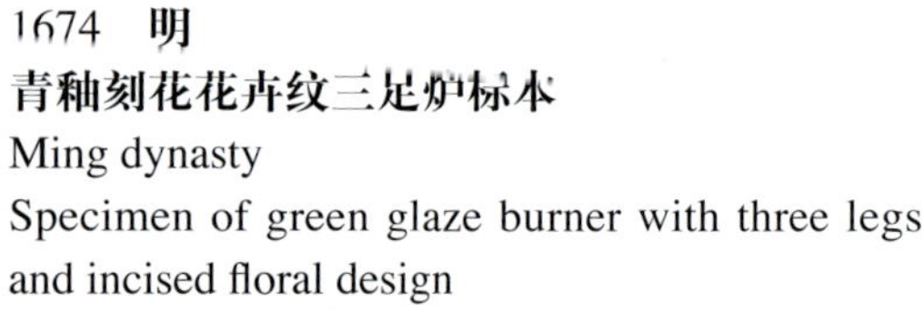

1674 **明**

**青釉刻花花卉纹三足炉标本**

Ming dynasty

Specimen of green glaze burner with three legs and incised floral design

1675　明

**青釉刻花花叶纹三足炉标本**

Ming dynasty

Specimen of green glaze burner with three legs and incised flower and leaf design

1676　明

**青釉刻花篦划花叶纹三足炉标本**

Ming dynasty

Specimen of green glaze burner with three legs and comb-incised flower and leaf design

1677　明　青釉刻花菊瓣纹碗标本

Ming dynasty

Specimens of green glaze bowl with incised design of chrysanthemum-petals

1678 **元至明 窑具标本**
From Yuan dynasty to Ming dynasty
Specimens of kiln furniture

1679 **元至明 窑具标本**
From Yuan dynasty to Ming dynasty
Specimen of kiln furniture

# 窑址考察论文选

## Selected Papers on Kiln Investigations

# 调查浙江鄞县窑址的收获

李辉柄

## 一 前言

鄞县窑址是浙江省文物管理委员会于 1958 年发现的。是继上虞窑、寺前窑之后又一重要发现，它为我们了解浙江地区青瓷的发展提供了新的资料，特别是对研究五代至北宋越窑具有十分重要的意义。

1963 年 10 月，笔者对浙江鄞县窑址进行了一次实地调查。在赴鄞县之前，观看了浙江省文物管理委员会采集的标本，无论从胎质、釉色，还是造型、纹饰等多方面观察，属于越窑系统是无疑的。它的产品较之受余姚上林湖影响的上虞、黄岩、东阳等窑为精，与余姚上林湖越窑的作风最为相似，甚至乍一看很难把它们区分开来。因此，鄞县窑与余姚上林湖越窑的关系之密切，以及它在越窑系统中的重要地位就不难想见了。

基于这种初步的印象，通过这次调查，一方面想尽可能地初步弄清鄞县窑的基本面貌和它烧瓷的历史；另一方面，想在获得大量材料的基础上进而探讨一下它与余姚上林湖越窑的关系——它们之间究竟是谁影响谁，以及它们各自的特点所在。然而这些绝不是通过一次调查所能解决的问题。大量的研究工作还有待于将来大面积发掘之后。

鄞县窑遗址面积很大，主要分布在鄞县南部东钱湖西南的郭家峙，东部的沙叶河头和小白市三处[1]。这三处窑址烧制器物大体相同，我们选择了郭家峙与小白市两地为重点进行了调查。现将这些材料加以综合整理，作为资料提供给大家研究。

## 二 标本整理与器物分类

这次调查共采集器物标本及窑具二百余片。器物有碗、盘、杯、罐、瓶、壶、钵、盏托、印盒、供器等多种，以碗为最多，盘次之，窑具有匣钵及大小垫圈等。

**（一）器物**

**1. 碗**

共有 17 式：

Ⅰ式。敞口外撇，口以下渐内收，高圈足微外撇，满釉，足内较深而底中心凸起。高 4.7 厘米，口径 11 厘米，足径 4.1 厘米。

Ⅱ式。敞口，口以下弧线内收，高圈足微外撇，满釉，足内较深而中心平坦。高 4.2 厘米，口径 10.7 厘米，足径 4.2 厘米。

Ⅲ式。浅形，敞口，口以下内收，器身弧度小，圈足外卷，满釉，底中心平坦。一种高 3.4 厘米，口径 13 厘米，足径 6.7 厘米；另一种高 3.2 厘米，口径 13.7 厘米，足径 7.2 厘米。

Ⅳ式。浅形，敞口，近底处稍丰，碗心内凹一圆形，圈内有划花纹饰，圈足外卷，满釉，底中心平坦。高 4.3 厘米，口径 12.6 厘米，足径 7.3 厘米。

Ⅴ式。敞口微撇，内口沿起线一圈，口以下弧线内收，矮圈足，满釉，底中心微凸起。高 4.4 厘米，口径 13 厘米，足径 5.3 厘米。

Ⅵ式。深形，敞口，器身弧度小，矮圈足，满釉，底中心平坦。一种高 4.8 厘米，口径 12.7 厘米，足径 5.1 厘米；另一种碗心微凸起，底中心微内凹，高 5.2 厘米，口径 13.8 厘米，足径 5.6 厘米。

Ⅶ式。敞口微撇，口以下弧线内收，器身留有明显的轮旋痕迹，近底处胎较厚，碗心内凹一圆形，圈足，满釉，底中心微凸。高 5.6 厘米，口径 14.2 厘米，足径 6.8 厘米。

Ⅷ式。敞口微撇，口以下弧线内收，碗心有划花纹饰，圈足矮浅，满釉，底中心微凸起。高 6 厘米，口径 15 厘米，足径 5.6 厘米。

Ⅸ式。深形，敞口，器身弧度小，留有明显的轮旋痕迹，碗心内凹一圈形，圈足，满釉，底中心平坦。高 6.3 厘米，口径 13.5 厘米，足径 6.3 厘米。

Ⅹ式。直口，底部丰满，形近似墩子，器身留有明显的轮旋痕迹，碗心内凹一圈形，高圈足，满釉，底中心平坦。高 7 厘米，口径 14 厘米，足径 6.8 厘米。

Ⅺ式。撇口，口以下弧线内收，器身压成花瓣形，碗心内凹一圈形，圈足，满釉，底中心平坦。高 5.2 厘米，口径 11.7 厘米，足径 5.4 厘米。同式碗有稍大者，碗心有划花纹饰，高 6.8 厘米，口径 13.8 厘米，足径 7.2 厘米。

Ⅻ式。浅形，口外撇，口以下弧形内收，器身压成花瓣形，碗心内凹一圈形，圈足高而壁厚，底中心微凸起。高 5.3 厘米，口径 14.2 厘米，足径 5.5 厘米。

ⅩⅢ式。直口，底部丰满，形近似墩子，器身压成花瓣形，碗心内凹一圈形，圈内有划花纹饰，高圈足微撇，满釉，底中心微凸起。高 7.2 厘米，口径 14 厘米，足径 7 厘米。

ⅩⅣ式。浅形，撇口，口以下弧线内收，碗内划荷叶形纹，圈足外卷，满釉，底中心微凸起。高 3.5 厘米，口径 14 厘米，足径 7 厘米。

ⅩⅤ 式。浅形，敞口，器身弧度小，碗心刻莲瓣纹，圈足，足上宽下窄，足内浅底中心微凸起。高 4 厘米，口径 13.5 厘米，足径 5.9 厘米。

ⅩⅥ 式。浅形，敞口，口以下弧线内收，碗心刻莲瓣纹，圈足外卷，满釉，底中心凸起。一种高 5.8 厘米，口径 19 厘米，足径 8.8 厘米，另一种高 5.6 厘米，口径 18.2 厘米，足径 8 厘米。

ⅩⅦ 式。折沿，口以下弧线内收，器身外部刻莲瓣纹，圈足微撇，底中心微凸起。高 5.4 厘米，口径 18 厘米，足径 8.4 厘米。

2. 盘

多无口，不能复原，盘心多为划花纹饰，有鹦鹉、蝴蝶与各种花草等。

3. 杯

有四式：

Ⅰ式。直口，器身弧度大，杯心有划花纹饰，圈足高而外卷，满釉，底中心微凹入。高 4.5 厘米，口径 8.8 厘米，足径 4.4 厘米。

Ⅱ式。造型与Ⅰ式杯相同，器身压成花瓣形，杯里刻划莲花纹。高 4.5 厘米，口径 8.8 厘米，足径 4.4 厘米；另一种稍浅，底部厚重，器里有划花纹饰。高 4.5 厘米，口径 9 厘米，足径 5 厘米。

Ⅲ式。因多无口不能复原，但能大体辨别出造型。此式杯有大小之分，制作精细，器身刻划莲瓣纹，圈足高而外卷，满釉。

4. 钵

有两式：

Ⅰ式。敛口，口以下弧线内收，器身刻三层莲花瓣纹，卧足，满釉，足内浅平。高 8 厘米，口径 19.5 厘米，足径 8.4 厘米；另一种器形与Ⅰ式钵相同，器身光素无纹。

Ⅱ式。卷口，口以下渐广，至腹部内收，平底，造型与五代余姚窑钵相同。

5. 罐

有两式：

Ⅰ式。敛口，罐体呈球形，周身刻划莲瓣纹，圈足，足内浅平。罐有盖，盖面刻有莲瓣纹饰，盖口合于罐口之中。通高 13 厘米，口径 6 厘米，腹径 14 厘米，足径 7.3 厘米。

Ⅱ式。直口，口以下渐广至底部内收，器身刻划四层莲瓣纹饰，圈足，底中心平坦。高 11.5 厘米，口径 11 厘米，足径 7 厘米。

6. 盏托

有两式：

Ⅰ式。盏面平坦，中心划有卷枝花卉纹饰，盏身刻莲瓣纹一周。托为板沿，沿面划有花草 10 枝，折腹，圈足高而外撇，底心空，满釉。高 3 厘米，口径 13 厘米，足径 8.2 厘米。

Ⅱ式。盏口微敛，口以下微广至腹部内收与托相连，托为碗形，圈足高而底中心平坦，满釉。高 5.5 厘米，盏口径 7.8 厘米，托口径 14 厘米，足径 5.5 厘米。

7. 洗

直口，卧足，洗内凸起。高 3 厘米，口径 11 厘米，足径 8.2 厘米。

8. 供器

敞口，口与身相连，器身上宽下窄，圈足，底中心空，周身深刻曲线纹饰。高 5 厘米，口径 15 厘米，足径 14 厘米。

9. 壶

都不能复原，从许多标本上看，壶多为撇口，长颈，椭圆腹，圈足。器身作瓜棱形，在腹的三分之一处，一面立壶嘴，一面立柄至颈部，肩部嘴与柄相等处立两个小圈形系，有的腹部还刻划各种纹饰。

10. 瓶

撇口，短颈，溜肩，肩以下渐广至腹部内收，在肩的对等处立两个细桥形系，胎厚重，器身有明显的轮旋痕迹，圈足，满釉，足内浅，底中心微凸起。高 17 厘米，口径 7.5 厘米，足径 6.2 厘米。

11. 盒

浅形，子口，卧足，盒心凸起。高 2 厘米，口径 10.5 厘米，底径 8.7 厘米。

（二）窑具

窑具有匣钵及大小垫圈等。

## 三　鄞县窑瓷器的造型及纹饰

辨别一种器物是否实用美观，首先要看到的是它的造型，其次才是它的釉色及纹饰。鄞县窑的制瓷艺人们很注重器物的造型与花纹装饰，并且把这两者巧妙地结合了起来，这可说是它的一个基本特征。

（一）造型

鄞县窑器物的成型，是有它一定规律的。例如碗的造型，基本上可分为两种：一种为深形，一种为浅形。深形碗大都口径是足径的一倍，足径恰好是碗的高度，如Ⅸ式、Ⅹ式、Ⅺ式、Ⅻ式碗等，就是按这种比例成型的。其他碗的成型，规律也大体如此。浅形碗的口径大于足径的一倍，足径的二分之一是碗的高度。如Ⅲ式、XIV式、XVI式碗等。杯的成型规律与深形碗相同，如Ⅰ式、Ⅱ式杯。盘的成型，虽然我们没有找到一件能够复原的标本，但根据上述三种器物成型的规律来推测，可能是足径加大一倍就是它的口径。

根据这种成型比例，可以了解鄞县窑的拉坯成型技术已达到相当高的水平。从大量标本中能够复原的数十种器物看，由于成型的比例适合，它给人以匀称协调之感，既实用而又美观。这些都构成了鄞县窑瓷器造型上的一个特征。

**（二）烧制方法**

一般地说是一件器物用一个匣钵，垫圈都支在器物的底部，所以器物的底部都留有支烧痕，圈足满釉，器里光滑。这样处理的结果，增加了器物的美观，同时提高了它的使用价值。

**（三）装饰方法**

有划花、刻花、刻划并用三种，以划花最为普遍。纹饰题材有鹦鹉、蝴蝶、莲瓣、莲花、水草，还有一些不易识别的花卉纹饰。

1. 划花

线条精细，刚劲有力，一般用在盘、碗、杯的装饰上。常见的盘心划双鹦鹉纹饰，头相对，尾相连，构成一幅完整的图案。有的划一只鹦鹉穿花；有的划双蝶展翅飞翔；也有随意几笔勾划出的水草、花卉，线条都很流利自然。碗心的装饰也多采用划花的方法，纹饰题材以叶纹居多，构图一般用叶茎把图案分成二等分，然后两边对称地划出叶或果构成一幅圆形图案。杯心的装饰与碗相同，划花线条非常熟练，多数只划一支花卉。

2. 刻花

线条粗壮有力，采用此种方法能使花纹凸起，给人以浮雕的感觉。这种装饰方法多用在罐、钵、壶等立体器物上。花纹题材以莲瓣纹为主。也有刻花与划花同时并用，以增加艺术效果。其做法是先刻好莲瓣主体纹饰以后，再用划花的方法划出花瓣茎。莲瓣有一层至四层不等，多数莲瓣层次分明，形象逼真。

一种器物使用什么方法对它进行装饰，造型和纹饰如何结合，是鄞县窑的匠师们非常注意的一个问题。我们从一件刻莲花纹盖罐可以看出艺人们的创造力。在球形罐的周身刻以莲瓣纹，使整个器物的造型就好像一朵未开的莲花一样。把器形与花纹巧妙地结合起来是鄞县窑的一种成功装饰。同时我们又可以看到用同样的方法装饰在不同造型的器物上，它的效果又各有所不同。一件刻莲花直口罐就是一个例子，它仿佛像一朵半开的莲花。再如刻莲花纹浅形碗，整个器形又成了一朵盛开的莲花。这几种器物之所以有这样好的艺术效果，是由于制瓷艺人们善于观察与掌握植物的形态，同时又成功地把器物的造型与纹饰很好地结合了起来。

## 四　鄞县窑与余姚上林湖越窑的关系

浙江是我国青瓷的主要发源地之一，著名的越窑就是其中的一支。

近几年来，经过多次调查，证明文献上所记载的越窑瓷器就出自余姚上林湖一带。越窑历史悠久，产品制作精巧，深受国内外人们的喜爱。远在唐代就置官监窑，为宫廷烧造所谓进御器物。唐代文人歌咏越窑瓷器的记载很多。到了五代，吴越钱镠家族统治的苏南、浙江，境内比较安定，经济有所发展，海外贸易也相应地扩大。吴越钱氏为维持自己的统治，不断向建立在中原地区的各王朝进贡。据文献记载，在开宝、太平兴国时期曾九次向宋朝贡，其中瓷器一项数量就达 21 万件以上。钱氏需要如此大量的贡物，光靠余姚上林湖一处烧窑是不可能达到的。那么这些贡瓷的产地又在哪里？鄞县窑遗址的发现，提供了新的资料。鄞县在唐时为鄞州，后改为明州。在《宋会要辑稿》“番夷七・历代朝贡”里有这样一段记载，明确提到明州贡瓷：开宝九年六月四日，“明州节度使惟治进……瓷器万一千事，内千事银棱。”据此，证明吴越钱氏的大量贡瓷中，一部分是属于鄞县窑的产品。

鄞县在浙江东部，位于钱塘江口的南岸，在唐和五代时，它是对外贸易的重要港口。钱氏用于海外贸易物中，除了金、银、缗钱、铅、锡、绢帛、绫锦等以外，瓷器也是当时的主要输出品之一。吴越钱氏在鄞县设窑，仿效余姚上林湖越窑的形制烧制瓷器，顺港出口较余姚更为便利。调查材料也证明，鄞县窑所烧制的器物无论在造型、胎质、釉色或是纹饰风格上，都与余姚上林湖越窑基本相同。因此，鄞县窑瓷器当时被用来大量出口是无疑的。

从以上情况来看，鄞县窑与其说是受余姚上林湖越窑的影响，还不如说它是从余姚上林湖越窑派生出来的另一支更为确切一些。

## 五　鄞县窑与余姚上林湖越窑的区别

基于上述两窑的这种关系，鄞县窑与余姚上林湖窑的产品有很多共同的地方是很自然的，但它们之间也还存在许多不同之点，主要有以下三个方面：

**（一）烧制品种和形制上的区别**

鄞县窑以生产碗、盘、杯、盏托等一类圆器为主，壶、瓶、罐、钵等立体器物较少。余姚窑烧制品种繁多，除了生产盘、碗、杯等器物以外，还有各式壶、瓶、罐、钵、洗、盒等。甚至五代至北宋这一时期的各种器形，几乎应有尽有。在形制上，一般余姚窑制作精细、规整，鄞县窑略为逊色。碗的形制除Ⅱ式、Ⅲ式、Ⅵ式、Ⅹ式碗与余姚窑基本相同外，一般鄞县窑碗的圈足较高而窄，底中心留有支烧痕；余姚窑碗的圈足矮而微宽，足上留有支烧痕。花瓣形碗，鄞县窑只压成线，口呈圆形；余姚窑压成线，口呈花瓣形。

### （二）胎釉上的区别

一般地讲，鄞县窑的胎质不如余姚窑坚硬，瓷化程度也较差。因此，余姚窑胎重，叩音清脆；反之，鄞县窑胎较轻，叩音稍差。鄞县窑窑火也不如余姚窑控制好，所以釉色不够稳定，那种所谓“秘色”（青绿色釉）较之余姚窑为少，而闪青黄釉的器物则较多，并且都有细小的开片。

### （三）装饰方法与纹饰上的区别

在装饰方法上，两窑虽然都有划花、刻花、刻划并用三种方法，并且都以划花为主，但是余姚窑所具有的印花、贴花、镂空等多种方法在鄞县窑遗址的标本中却很少见到。在纹饰题材上，鄞县窑也不如余姚窑丰富多彩，除两窑共有的纹饰如鹦鹉、蝴蝶、荷叶莲花、海水、花草以外，余姚窑还有人物、云鹤、云龙、飞凤、各种鸟兽以及牡丹等多种，这些在鄞县窑遗址中尚未发现。总的来说，余姚窑的纹饰一般较之鄞县窑清晰，线条流畅。

另外，虽然两窑同用一种纹饰题材装饰，但在画法上也不尽相同。例如常见的鹦鹉纹饰就是如此。头部的画法，鄞县窑头肥大，余姚窑较瘦长；鹦鹉翅的画法两窑都为三层，鄞县窑翅的第二层为双线，余姚窑则为单线；鄞县窑鹦鹉的眼眶为一弧线，眼珠为三角线，余姚窑眼眶为一弧线，眼珠为圆圈；鄞县窑鹦鹉头上不戴花，而余姚窑戴花者居多。双蝴蝶的画法也有类似的情况。头部的画法，鄞县窑中心画一圈，余姚窑画三角线或不画线；鄞县窑蝶须长直，余姚窑须短而卷；鄞县窑蝶翅尖长而上卷，余姚窑圆而不上卷；余姚窑蝶颈与头不连，以曲线分开，鄞县窑颈与头相连；蝶尾的画法也不相同。

## 六　结语

鄞县窑的发现，充实了越窑的内容，鄞县窑产品在质量上虽然不如余姚上林湖越窑的精致，但比上虞、黄岩等窑为佳。

最后提一下鄞县窑烧瓷的历史。据明嘉靖《宁波府志·山川》记载：“鄞县……省窑山横山东三里许，邑鄮时尝作陶于此，故名……”鄞县汉时称鄮县，隋代入句章，唐代又恢复鄮县，五代梁时改为鄞县。据此，鄞县窑至少应在唐代以前就开始烧瓷了。在调查小白市遗址时，发现有东晋时的瓷片与窑具，形制与萧山上董窑、德清窑相似。南朝时期常见的一种碗形标本也有发现。这就说明鄞县在东晋时代已开始烧窑，到了南朝时期还继续烧造，这与上述文献记载是相符的。但是，从我们在郭家峙、小白市的所有遗址中采集的标本来看，除了上述早期遗物以外，其余全部是属于五代至北宋时期的遗物，而唐代的遗物却未发现。可能鄞县窑在这一时期已经停烧，到了五代，由于吴越钱氏为了进贡和海外贸易的特殊需要，必须扩大生产范围，因之，除余姚上林湖外，在许多地方还设立了新窑，鄞县窑于此时才又恢复了生产。由于余姚上林湖越窑在当时所获得的声誉，所建新窑势必按照它的形制来进行生产，鄞县窑只是其中的一个，估计类似的窑址今后还可能在这一带陆续被发现。

注释：

1 浙江省文物管理委员会：《浙江鄞县古瓷窑址调查记要》，《考古》1964 年第 4 期。

# The Results of Investigation of Yinxian Kiln Sites in Zhejiang Province

Li Huibing

Yinxian kiln was found in 1958. Kiln sites were widely distributed in Yinxian County, mainly in the south and the east. The author carried out an investigation into Yinxian kiln sites at Guojiazhi and Xiaobaishi, Yinxian County, Zhejiang Province in October, 1963. Based on specimens collected, Yinxian kiln wares are very much similar to those of Yueyao kiln in term of body texture, glaze, shaping and decoration style. It is no doubt that it belongs to the Yueyao Kiln System. Major types are bowls, plates, cups, jars, vases, pots, alms bowls, saucers, boxes, sacrificial wares, etc. Of which, bowl is maximum in number, followed by plate. This paper focuses on the introduction and description of various types of celadon of the kiln. It also deals with the shaping and decorative features of Yinxian kiln wares and the relationship between Yinxian kiln and Yueyao kiln. A comparative study, i.e. similarities and differences on the decorative patterns shared by the two kilns, such as parrots and butterflies, was conducted by the author. The finding of Yinxian kiln provided us with new information to understand the celadon development in Zhejiang Province. In particular, it is of importance for the study of history and scope of Yueyao kiln from Five Dynasties to Northern Song dynasty.

# 浙江象山唐代青瓷窑址调查

李知宴

1974年10月5日，浙江省文物管理委员会、象山县文化馆、中国历史博物馆、故宫博物院等单位的同志，在象山港距出海口不远的地方，发现一处唐代初期的青瓷窑址，并对该窑址进行了现场勘察。窑场遗址出土的器物在造型、装饰、制作工艺、生产时代以及在东海之滨的地理位置等特点，对研究我国古代沿海地区瓷器生产情况和发展历史，都提供了有价值的资料。现将有关资料和初步分析报告如下。

## 一　窑址的地理环境

象山青瓷窑址位于象山县城东北面的黄避岙公社鲁家岙大队，在黄大山脚下塔曼礁西边的一个山丘上，山丘坡度平缓，背靠大山，西边距象山港水面约200米，不远就是大海，山丘南边和西边是平地（今为稻田）。瓷片堆积层，根据实地测量，厚度达一米多，其面积东西达100多米，南北约60米。在这样的堆积层的四周，还有一些厚度不等的堆积。烧瓷的窑基就在山坡上。这次调查时发现龙窑的窑基一座，以后象山县文化馆的同志们又发现一座龙窑，找到窑门的基石。这两座龙窑，都是长约50米，宽5米。窑头朝西，在山坡的下端，窑尾朝东，在山坡的上头，依山筑窑。在窑身左侧露出一个圆形的原料加工场的平面，直径有20多米。现在是稻田的两块平地，当时可能是瓷窑作坊的建筑物所在地。把瓷片堆积层、窑床构筑范围、加工场地、建筑所在地连起来看，可能就是一个完整的的瓷窑作坊。在山丘西边大山脚下有一条人工挖掘的大沟，那里有灰白的瓷土露出，可能就是当年制瓷取土遗留下来的。

## 二　产品的种类和窑具

从窑址堆积物观察，该窑场产品种类比较单纯，造型古朴，釉色品种不多，装饰简单，窑具只有很原始的匣钵和垫饼两种。现在把采集的器物标本整理出来，供研究的同志参考。

### （一）器物

根据实物分析，有碗、盘、钵、瓶、罐等种。

1. 碗

在窑址堆积层中碗的残片极多，是所有器物中比例最大的一类，造型的基本特征为敛口，曲腹，平底，从细部特征分析可以分为三式：

Ⅰ式。口微敛，唇部较圆，曲腹，上腹微鼓，下腹瘦长，平底，器形比较小。高 4.6 厘米，口径 13.4 厘米，底径 6 厘米。

Ⅱ式。口微敛，尖唇，下腹较直，平底，器形比Ⅰ式为大。高 6.4 厘米，口径 17 厘米，底径 1.4 厘米。

Ⅲ式。直口，圆唇，上腹很浅，下腹曲度比较大，平底。高 6 厘米，口径 18 厘米，底径 8 厘米。

2. 盘

只见到一种盘的残体，盘口外侈，口沿较尖，盘体平坦而浅。经过比较分析，这种盘式属于高足盘。

3. 钵

钵的特征和碗基本一样，不同的是体形大，腹部很深，常见的有两种式样：

Ⅰ式。敛口，束颈，上腹微曲，下腹瘦长，小平底，体形比较大。高 9.6 厘米，口径 25.4 厘米，底径 9 厘米。

Ⅱ式。体形较大，敛口，平唇，束颈，上腹圆鼓，小平底，底心微凹。高 11 厘米，口径 32 厘米，底径 11 厘米。

4. 瓶

从造型特点看，可分为两式：

Ⅰ式。侈口，口沿外卷，尖唇，颈较长，口沿至肩安竖耳两个，斜肩，鼓腹，下腹瘦小。口径 10 厘米，颈壁厚约 1 厘米。

Ⅱ式。短颈，侈口，尖唇，丰肩，肩部横安双耳。口径 12.6 厘米，肩壁厚 0.6 厘米。

5. 罐

在窑址堆积中，罐的残片很多，从采集的标本看可以分为五式：

Ⅰ式。口沿微外卷，圆唇，短颈，颈肩之间一道深弦纹，丰肩。口沿至肩部的高度是 6.5 厘米，口径 15 厘米，器壁厚 0.7 厘米。

Ⅱ式。敛口，卷沿，圆尖唇，短颈，颈的曲度较大，丰肩，肩部横安双耳。口沿至肩部高 6 厘米，口径 15.6 厘米，器壁厚 0.6~0.8 厘米。

Ⅲ式。形体较小，卷沿，平口，尖唇，颈极短，在紧挨颈边的肩上安横耳，肩部很窄，由肩转向腹部的地方弧度极小，口沿至上腹高 5.4 厘米，壁厚 0.7~1 厘米。

Ⅳ式。直颈较短，口沿微外卷，丰肩，肩部安横耳，口沿至肩部高 7.1 厘米，颈长 2.2 厘米，壁厚 0.5~0.7 厘米。

Ⅴ式。短颈，口沿外卷，颈的下端突出一棱，丰肩。口沿至肩高 6.5 厘米，颈长 2 厘米，壁厚 0.5~0.8 厘米。

还有一些罐的残片，看不出器形的结构，只看见肩部耳的形式。

6. 瓮

瓷瓮的体形很大，器壁很厚，只发现一些下腹及底部的残片，腹壁很直，平底。较大的一片，下腹的高度为 18 厘米，壁厚为 1.5~3.5 厘米，底部厚度为 2.2 厘米。

**（二）窑具**

在窑场遗址的堆积中，窑具数量很多，但种类单调，只有匣钵和垫饼。

1. 匣钵

较大的高 19 厘米，腹径 11.6 厘米，壁厚 1~2.6 厘米；较小的高只有 10 厘米，壁厚 1.6~3 厘米。在匣钵的下部有对称的圆形或方形的小孔。

2. 垫饼

都是不规则的圆形，一般直径有 4.5 厘米，有的直径 3.6 厘米，有的很小，只有 2.5 厘米。厚度一般为 0.14~1.5 厘米不等。

匣钵和垫饼的使用：器物的坯体底部放着三个至四个不等的垫饼托着，再在垫饼下放一个器物，在匣钵里成叠地堆积起来，然后装窑。还发现有烧窑时发生窑粘和变形的成叠器物。

## 三 器物的造型和装饰特征

象山青瓷窑场生产的瓷器，造型古朴，结实，耐用。关于器形的设计，从大量的标本观察首先考虑的是实用。例如碗、钵一类形制大体相同的器物，有各种不同的型号，但一般口径和底径的比例都在三比一左右，即口径比底径大一倍半左右，腹部的线条有的曲度小，较直，有的曲度大，这是从器物大小不同考虑的，前者是较小的器物，后者是较大的器物，这样在使用时拿起来很顺手，放在平面上很平稳。罐、瓶类器物，在成型时也很注意各部分的比例，线条的弧度和转折，如瓶的结构，从瓶的颈部，往上线条缓缓外侈，到口沿时外卷，在颈的下端弧度变大，与腹部相接慢慢收小，这样颈部至口沿造型就很秀气。肩丰满，腹部圆鼓，下腹瘦长，看起来稳重。在肩部都安上粗壮的横式耳或双线条的竖耳，结实耐用。这些情况说明象山青瓷窑场工匠们创作的瓷器符合实用与美观相结合的工艺要求，造型艺术已经达到相当高的水平。

象山青瓷窑场的产品比较朴素，没有华贵和繁缛的装饰。可是，该窑瓷器上设计的大片彩色装饰，以及几种颜色相间调配起来的斑点和斑块装饰，却是我国青瓷装饰艺术中这类技巧最早的，它比河南郏县窑的彩斑装饰和湖南长沙窑的彩斑装饰都早得多，这一点值得特别注意。

象山窑青瓷的装饰有以下几种：

第一，在器物的颈部、肩部或腹部有一道至五道不等的线条组成的弦纹，有的上下起伏好像波浪一样，有的用篦齿状的工具划成篦纹。

第二，在青瓷的釉里，施以大片的酱色彩斑。这种彩斑的做法是：用含铁氧化物的矿物原料配成彩料，当坯体上釉并阴干以后，再把这种带彩的原料涂在釉上，入窑经过高温焙烤时，彩料和釉料熔融在一起，彩料高温熔融后流动，在器物上出现大片彩斑，这些彩斑深浅不同，相间排列，收到优美的艺术效果。

第三，用金属铁的成分不同的化合物，如三氧化二铁（$Fe_2O_3$)、氧化亚铁（FeO) 等配成彩料，用笔蘸着彩料在釉上点出各种小块斑点，经高温焙烤以后，这种彩料和釉熔融在一起，出现不同色彩的斑块或斑点，有的是酱色的，有的是褐色的，有的是浅黄色的，有的呈乳浊状的灰色蓝。这些斑点自然地排列起来，图案效果很好。

这些情况说明象山青瓷窑场工匠们比较好地掌握了金属氧化物在瓷器釉料和彩料中的呈色原理，成功地运用了线条和斑点的图案规律来装饰瓷器。

## 四　胎和釉的工艺特点

根据象山青瓷窑场产品的胎、釉观察，可以了解到该窑场瓷器制作的一些工艺成就和特点。象山窑青瓷的胎体有的是灰白色，有的是黄褐色或褐红色。灰白色胎体比较坚硬、细致，烧结程度比较好，在放大镜下能看到发亮的光泽，没有很大的泡孔或断裂。这类瓷器成品说明该窑工匠的制瓷技巧是比较高的，只能在选料、淘洗、捏练、陈腐等工艺过程中操作比较熟练，要求比较严格的情况下才能做到。

黄褐色或褐红色一类器物的胎体比较厚，胎泥颗粒比较粗糙，结构比较疏松，有较大的孔隙和断裂，烧结程度比较低，而胎体在塑造过程中也有厚薄不均的现象，所以在烧窑时，胎体受高热就会出现因器物各部分荷重软化情况不一致而产生的变形，该窑场不少产品就是因为这个缘故而报废的。

施釉情况，盘、钵一类器物只施在口沿部分，罐、瓶一类器物只施在口沿到上腹部分，其余部分均露胎，只有极个别的器物内壁施釉。

釉层比较厚，釉质比较细腻莹润，光泽很好。这些釉是属于石灰质的高温玻璃釉。青绿色的呈色剂是金属铁的氧化物，是用还原火焰烧成的。色调较深，青翠美观。有的釉色呈青灰色，青中泛白，颜色较淡，光泽不如前种。还有青黄色釉，青中泛黄，釉层较薄，纹片很细。还有一种酱色釉，在器物表面不均匀，呈麻癞斑状。这种现象出现的原因较多，一般来说如果釉浆存放时间过长，或配料时釉浆过稠，施在器物表面后，受热时熔融不充分，瓷器上就会出现这种不均匀的麻癞斑块。

另外，在部分瓷器釉面上，局部地方呈现出乳浊色的钧釉现象。这种现象是焙烤瓷器时，由于还原火焰控制不好，釉料中氧化亚铁的乳浊作用产生的。有的器物由于挂釉薄厚不均匀，在釉层的边缘有蜡泪状的流釉，有的器物釉层和胎体密合得不好而致使釉层剥落。

## 五　关于时代的识认和该窑发现的重要意义

我们认为象山县黄避岙青瓷窑生产的时代应该是唐代初期。这是根据调查中得到的标本分析的，其理由是：

第一，典型器物的造型特征普遍具有唐代初期瓷器的风格。如高足盘，这种器物是北朝、南朝、隋、初唐时期的作品。唐代中期墓葬里就见不到了。象山窑出土的高足盘瓷片的特点是隋到初唐时期的，它与安阳仁寿三年卜仁墓里出土的高足盘特点很接近。罐类器物短颈，口微侈，卷沿，圆唇或尖圆唇。钵类器物敛口，平底，腹部较直，口和底直径的比例一般是二比一左右。器物比较单纯，都是唐代早期瓷器的特点。

第二，该窑场器物上的釉是青绿色的高温釉。碗、盘、钵一类器物只施在口沿部分，瓶、罐、瓮一类器物只施在口沿至上腹，大部分胎体不施釉，装饰比较简单，这些特点是唐代器物施釉的特点。

第三，在堆积的瓷片中有不少器物的附件如横式耳、竖式耳、复式双耳等都是很经典的唐代早期瓷器的特点。

第四，匣钵和垫饼都是用同样的原料做成的，即用褐色耐火泥做成，里面含有粗沙，焙烤以后匣钵坯体起了很多像蜂窝状的泡孔。垫饼呈不规则的圆形，几乎是随便一捏便用。然而，这些窑具的原料和瓷器坯体原料完全不同。窑具和瓷器原料相差很大，两者原料的物理性质不同，在受窑火焙烤或冷却时，其膨胀和收缩系数不同，致使瓷器容易发生变形或窑裂现象，直接影响到瓷器的成品率。这种窑具也是比较早的。我们看到浙江南部丽水县的吕步坑窑址中出土的窑具以及使用方法与象山青瓷窑址中的窑具基本一样。吕步坑窑址的瓷器上限到南朝，下限到唐初。

关于象山瓷窑，古代文献上有所记载。这些记载基本都是根据明曹昭《格古要论》的描写而来的。这些记载都说象山瓷窑是宋代的，其特点是“色白滋润者高，色黄而质粗者低”。我们这次调查没有看到宋代瓷窑，尤其是宋代的白瓷窑。这次发现的唐代初期青瓷窑场遗址，根据它的地理环境，远离城镇，在象山港的海边，不远就是大海，背面是延绵不断的大山环绕。工匠们来到这个地方，就地取材，用本地瓷土和烧之不尽的木柴，从人们生活实际需要出发，烧出结实耐用的瓷器。然而，窑场附近人烟稀少，有大山相隔，与内地城镇交通十分不便。可能窑场范围不小，堆积层也比较厚，估计生产规模不会很小。生产的成品，当地居民只能实用一部分，大部分利用便利的海路交通运往外地销售。从其经营性质来说，这个窑场是民间作坊，生产的瓷器主要是为了外销，可以用船运往我国沿海城镇销售，也可以输出到海外。在瓷窑附近的海滩上，我们看到不少的瓷器碎片，有的就泡在海水里，这可能就是装船时损坏而遗留下来的。

东海之滨唐代初期青瓷窑址的发现，在全国来说是第一次。这在我国瓷器研究上有重要的意义。同时，在我国沿海地区和海岛的领土上，不断有古代各个时期的瓷器出土，这个窑址的发现为我们分析判断这些出土瓷器的产地和窑址提供了极好的资料。

瓷器是我国古代传统的外销产品。在我国与世界各国经济、文化交流中起了重要的作用。在朝鲜、日本以及南亚、西亚、非洲、欧洲各地都发现了各个时代的瓷器。这个唐代初期以外销为主的窑址的发现，也为研究我国古代外销瓷器增添了资料。

象山窑在我国古代是一个有重要影响的窑场，关于它的产品在不少文献里有记载，如《格古要论》、《留留青》、《事物绀珠》、《瓶史》、《砚山斋杂记》、《景德镇陶录》、《陶说》等。这些文献都说是宋代开始的。这次唐代初期青瓷窑址的发现将象窑的历史提前了将近三个世纪，说明象山地方烧瓷历史十分悠久，这个窑址的发现对研究唐代瓷窑概况和沿海地区瓷器生产状况都有重要的意义。

# The Investigation of A Tang Dynasty Celadon Kiln Site in Xiangshan County, Zhejiang Province

Li Zhiyan

On October 5, 1974, experts from the Committee for Cultural Relics Management of Zhejiang Province, the Cultural Center of Xiangshan County, the Historical Museum of China, the Palace Museum and other units found an early Tang dynasty celadon kiln site by the Xiangshan Harbour. Then, the experts carried out on-site investigation. Unearthed artifacts are bowls, plates, alms bowls, jars, vases, urns with relatively rough and thick body, darker glaze and simple decoration and kiln furniture as well. Simple decoration is meant for strings, comb-incised patterns and brown splashes which vary in sizes, from big spots to small dots. The decorative style of those unearthed artifacts is very much similar to that of wares of the time across Zhejiang Province. Unearthed artifacts, in term of shaping, decoration, production technique, production time and location by the East China Sea, etc., are valuable reference for the study of ancient coastal porcelain production and the history of porcelain development of China.

# 浙江龙泉青瓷山头窑发掘的主要收获

李知宴

1979年4月，浙江省文物管理委员会、上海博物馆、考古所、中国历史博物馆、故宫博物院等单位组成紧水滩工程考古队，共同对龙泉青瓷窑址进行了发掘。根据各单位发掘资料自行整理、自行发表的原则，现将故宫博物院发掘的这一部分的主要收获介绍如下，供研究龙泉青瓷的同志们参考。

## 一　勘察与发掘

故宫博物院考古组发掘的窑址编号为79龙BY12，即龙泉青瓷窑址B区第12号窑。该窑窑址在龙泉雁川公社大白岸的山头窑村，该窑是山头窑群中的一个。5月5日开始发掘，6月18日结束，历时24天。

窑址位置在山坡上，从溪水旁边算起，处于第三层坡地上，方向北偏东41度，浙江考古队发掘的13号窑在它的上面一层台地上，14号窑在对面山坡上，西北方向的山坡上还有两座窑。几座窑中间有一块稻田，此外，每座窑附近都有一块平地。这些稻田和平地当年可能是瓷窑的作坊工场所在，这块田地没有进行发掘。

窑基的左边有大量自然形成的灰白色风化黏土，颗粒较细，似为烧瓷的原料。这里满山树林、草丛和毛竹，可作烧窑的燃料，坡下便是一条溪流，因此在这里建窑是很理想的。

## 二　窑址堆积和窑炉结构

### （一）窑址堆积

这里的表层土的厚度分别为20厘米、30厘米、50厘米、100厘米不等，少数地段表面露出红烧土块，堆积很薄。窑床尾部堆积厚达140～150厘米左右。表土层为灰黑和深黑泥土、红色碎块、碎瓷片、废匣钵、垫饼和垫圈等，现代遗物极少。说明该窑废弃以后自然倒塌，很少扰乱。表土层下是红烧土层（即砌窑用的红砖和土坯，经窑火焙烧以后变成的红色硬块），厚度10～40厘米不等。揭开此层便是窑炉的拱顶层，只有一层砖的厚度，为窑炉倒塌的原始痕迹。以下是窑底层，出土匣钵、烧坏了的器物、烧不成熟的坯件、碎瓷片等，堆积厚度不匀，有的匣钵成叠堆积在一起。窑尾部分的匣钵里还有完整的器物。

窑底下面是红褐色沙砾层，夯筑结实。

### （二）窑炉结构

该窑顺坡而筑，窑头在下部，窑尾在上部，斜坡长度为62.6米，水平长度为58.6米。

#### 1. 窑头

较小，半圆形，前部较尖，后部较宽，炉膛高26厘米，长86厘米，宽为150厘米。里面有砖砌的通气孔道，孔道的上部用圆形的匣钵底片盖着，用长20厘米，前宽16厘米，后宽18厘米的楔形砖砌成。

#### 2. 窑床

从窑头末端一道横墙算起，往上面5米处的一段窑床，用红色楔形砖砌成，再上用废匣钵砌成窑墙，匣钵都是直径28～30厘米的大型匣钵，砌好以后抹涂厚约5厘米的耐火泥，窑墙厚33～35厘米。耐火泥掺有较粗的沙砾，经高温焙烤以后颜色为紫褐色。窑床紧挨窑头部分的宽度为150～164厘米，中部最宽部分为210厘米。12号窑窑床右侧（东边）是一层匣钵砌成的墙，窑墙后面是用石头砌成的宽210厘米左右的路面，窑床内壁的熔结面很厚，坚硬而光亮，很多匣钵被烧裂；左侧（西边）是匣钵砌成的双层墙，墙面抹涂的耐火黏土只有轻微的烧熔，打开第一层匣钵墙，第二层匣钵墙的情况和第一层一样，也有轻微的烧熔，说明紧靠窑墙里壁的这一道墙是后续上去的。所以，它的烧熔面就没有右侧那样强烈。

#### 3. 窑顶

窑顶几乎全部倒塌，在窑床上堆积成一层红砖，有的地方大面积保存倒塌的原样。经过清理，可以看到窑顶的砌筑结构。即在匣钵砌成的墙面上，用红色楔形砖铺砌二层，形成平坦而坚固的平面，再用长18.5厘米，宽13厘米，厚5.8厘米的红砖从窑床两边的墙面起坡，至顶面起券而成。从窑尾保留的一部分未下塌的窑顶看，窑顶构筑比较平缓。

#### 4. 窑尾

窑床从50米以后宽度逐渐缩小为200至210厘米。窑尾开始砌横墙，尾墙以后再延长80厘米，砌垒一堵石头墙，用以挡火。窑尾墙由底向上先砌六个匣钵柱，高44～46厘米不等。匣钵柱之间有七个排气孔，在上面用匣钵相错排列砌墙，墙顶上有五个圆圈形排气孔。使用时，如墙下的排气孔够用，上面的排气孔就用瓦片盖住，如下面排气孔不足以排气，则打开上面的排气孔，使烟气畅通。窑尾顶部两侧，各有一方形孔，是用来观察窑尾部分的火焰情况，或取照子（试火板）用的。这样的结构在今天民间龙窑中仍然存在。

5. 窑门

共有 13 个结构清楚的窑门，还有一个窑门被扰乱坑所破坏，窑门两侧的柱子是用直径 28 厘米的匣钵由下而上砌起来的，窑门均在窑床右侧。第一号窑门距离窑头 2.98 米，最后一号窑门即第 14 号窑门距离窑头 55.92 米。每个窑门之间的距离 3～4.6 米不等。窑门的宽度 0.4～0.5 米不等。由于顶部下塌，窑门的高度不详，残高有 1.15 米，最矮只剩 0.3 米。窑门的建筑材料一般用匣钵和红砖。封门材料用砖、石头、废匣钵，有的一层砖，一层匣钵。窑门的深度 0.44～0.6 米，门槛分别用石头、大方砖、废匣钵修筑而成。只有第五号窑门剩下三层台阶。

6. 投柴孔

发现 16 个投柴孔的痕迹。在窑尾南边（右侧）的墙壁上还有两个相邻的投柴孔，在窑墙上砌成方斗形，外壁较敞，窑墙里面较窄，到墙里壁又较敞开。两个投柴孔相隔只有 0.5 米。在不远的地方还有两个。投柴孔在窑墙两侧设置，在左侧与南边投柴孔相对的位置也发现投柴孔的烧熔面，最后一个孔距 14 号窑门 1.06 米，离底部高 1.35 米，这个投柴孔底部宽 12 厘米，上部宽 7 厘米，高 7 厘米，也是方斗形。

7. 窑床底部

窑床底的结构是在生土层上有一层夹沙的泥土，约 18～20 厘米。经高温烧烤以后，其色调不一样，分灰黑色层、褐黄色沙层、紫红色沙层等。在这层夹沙土的上面，用匣钵铺地，有五个、六个、七个一排的，在一米的范围约三排，上面再置装有坯件的匣钵。

**（三）堆积层的清理**

在窑床的右侧平地和斜坡上堆积着瓷窑生产中的废品及用坏了的窑具等，清理时打了四个探方。

顺着窑墙与窑门垂直方向开探方。清理结果只能分出表土层和遗物层，深浅不一，以探方一为例，4×5 平方米，表土厚 26 厘米。清出遗物有划花碗 83 个、葵口碗 11 个、素面碗 44 个、小碗 11 个、盘 3 个、未烧好的半成品 11 个，还有看不出器形的葵瓣形瓷片 62 片、釉色和花纹都较好的瓷片 45 片、平底盘残片 3 片及其他瓷片 520 片。下层出土划花碗 38 个、素面碗 13 个、小碗 4 个、圈足盘 3 个及其他瓷片 20 片，这些出土的碎片和窑床出土的一样。其他三个探方打在斜坡堆积上，堆积厚一些，但堆积物没有什么不同。

## 三　青瓷种类和装饰艺术

**（一）器物种类**

这次发掘出丰富的标本，有罐、壶、瓶、碗、盏、盘、碟、杯、扣盒、药碾、照子（试火板）、轱镳轴碗等。其中以各种型号的碗、盘最多，大约占90%以上。该窑产品单纯，碗、盘类占的比例最大。这些器物的规格、特征、分类排比，计有：罐、壶（可分两式）、杯（可分两式）、钵、小盏（可分四式）、碗（可分12式）、盘（可分7式）、碾钵、扣盒、盒盖（有三种样式）、罐盖。

尚有工具如印花模子、轮箍、轴顶碗、试火碗、试火板等。

匣钵、垫饼和垫圈，这类工具很多，在窑址附近成堆出现。匣钵，可分为大、中、小三种类型。大型高7.5～9厘米，上径为27～29.5厘米，下径为26.5～27.8厘米，壁厚1～2厘米，耐火泥做成，结实，大部分保存完好，有的上面流淌有斑斑釉痕；中型一般直径为26.5厘米，厚1.5厘米；小型直径18～20厘米。中小型上径和下径相差2厘米左右，上大下小。

匣钵的顶面凹下，使用比较特别，垫饼和垫圈，也分大、中、小型，大的高3.2～3.5厘米，直径7.4～7.8厘米，厚1.2～1.5厘米，用粗瓷土做成，放在匣钵底部垫瓷器的坯件，有圆形、圆环形，很不规整，比较坚实。中型一般高1.2厘米，直径4.5厘米，厚1.1厘米；小型高0.8厘米，直径2.4～3.4厘米，厚0.5厘米，其余同上。

窑砖，砌窑墙、封门都使用了各种型号的砖。拱顶用楔形砖，红色或红黄色，长15～15.5厘米，宽前部为16～17厘米，后部14～15厘米，厚4.5～5.8厘米。质地松脆，保存不好，但用量很大。封门砖，有梯形、长方形。长方形一般长14～25厘米不等，宽7.5～9厘米，厚3.5～15.5厘米。

**（二）青瓷的装饰艺术**

是以刻花和划花为主。刻花是以犀利的刻刀刻划出生动活泼的写实图案。内容有花卉、水草、野草、浮萍、莲花、荷叶和水波纹，还有写实性很强的鱼纹、大雁纹等。其中，以莲花和水波纹为最多。划花是用很细的篦齿状工具在胎面划出平行线条的水波纹和云纹。刻花遒劲有力，划花细致纤巧。刻花多为装饰的主题纹样，划花多为陪衬内容，对主题花纹起到良好的烘托作用。最优美的花卉是在圆形盒盖上盛开的牡丹花纹，Ⅱ式盒盖上的牡丹花纹，花瓣舒展，花蕊突出，绿叶下垂于花下，衬托得花蕊花瓣极为美丽和华贵。

装饰花纹的内容，完全取材于生活，都是当时当地人们常见的、熟悉的东西，今天群众还能叫出名字来，如一种团形图案，群众称为“浮田萍”，在龙泉地区的水田、水塘里极多；一种野草群众称为“芋菜”，是一种苦菜，人可以吃，也可以喂猪；另一种五瓣形的团形图案，群众称为“扎菜”，是一种中草药，可以治病。

## 四　几点认识

**1. 关于该窑的生产时代**

发掘过程中发现不少带文字的瓷片资料，有“金玉满堂”、“蒋宅”、“林立”、“溪边泥”、“上”、“天下太平”等，但没有具体年款的文字，只能根据产品的特点来判断：

第一，产品是一般青瓷，釉层的玻璃质较强，釉色为青绿、灰绿、褐绿、黄绿等，釉层较薄。这是早期特征，不是南宋龙泉青瓷那种如美玉般的凝厚釉层。根据过去出土的龙泉青瓷中有绝对年代的资料来看，南宋、元、明各代均没有这些特征。

第二，其造型和装饰风格与北宋定窑、耀州窑有相同之点。如装饰技法以刻花和划花为主，水波组织和鱼儿图案组织在风格上相似。

第三，有不少小碗，平底，圆饼实足，这种碗形制较早。

第四，在窑床下部出土器物中也有一些侈口、深腹、平底、圈足的碗，胎体较白而细，釉色翠绿，质地光润，釉层较厚。以莲瓣作装饰，莲瓣的特点是修长，头部较尖瘦。

前三点是时代较早的特征，可以早到北宋，后一点是较晚的特征。还有“天下太平”这样的刻字。根据过去的经验，这类文字有和元丰年号同刻在一件器物上的。所以该窑生产时代断在北宋中晚期比较恰当。

**2. 该窑是龙窑构筑**

浙江地区就曾发现春秋战国时期的龙窑。我们发掘的龙窑相当完善，依山筑窑，斜度适中，中腰部分比较平缓，窑头有预热室，窑尾有排气孔和挡火墙。窑头横断面积最小，考虑到烧窑开始时需要热量最多。窑身中部最宽，热量易于集中。窑尾又较小，可以保持适当的动压。拱顶成弧形，两侧上部设有投柴孔，左侧有窑门，用于装坯和出窑。从窑床结构看，龙窑内各种阻力很小，主要靠坯件匣钵的装置作阻力。由于阻力小，外加的压头和气流的速度都可以小一些，而且易于达到平衡，不必采用辅助阻力。在热利用方面，有效地利用了烟气热量和产品吸收的热量，使废气热损降低至极小，提高燃烧温度。化学热损和机械热损都不大，使窑尾的预热带能维持不大的正压，不致吸入冷空气。

装坯情况，窑头多小碗、杯、盏、小盘，大型、中型碗数量较少。中部大型的罐、壶、碗数最多，小型器物较少。中后部大、中型碗均有，小盘、小盏、小碗很多，窑尾多半成品或焙烤的坯件。

这种瓷窑结构简单，多利用废匣钵砌墙，在古代手工生产的时代，设计和建筑都比较理想。窑的产量，估计为 18000 件左右，如果扣除窑门和投柴孔附近的空地，一窑可能生产成品达 15000 件左右。

**3. 釉色发灰、发黄**

质量较高的一类产品，胎质细，浅灰色，釉色比较青翠。大多数胎质颗粒较粗，没有采用捣碎原料的工序，将风化黏土淘洗后即进行制作。另外，龙窑窑体很长，不利于控制火焰，所以产品的釉色大部分都发灰或发黄。

# The Results of the Excavation of Longquan Celadon Kiln Site at Shantouyao, Zhejiang Province

Li Zhiyan

In April 1979, an archaeological team was organized by the Committee for Cultural Relics Management of Zhejiang Province, the Shanghai Museum, the Institute for Archaeological Research of Chinese Academy for Social Sciences, the Historical Museum of China, the Palace Museum and other units. The mission of the team is to excavate Longquan celadon kiln sites found at the construction site of the Jinshuitan Project. Experts from the Palace Museum excavated a kiln site called Shantouyao. It was a kiln in shape of a dragon and built along a slope. It consists of the front gate, the kiln bed and the bottom, the top of the kiln, the kiln door, the holes for sending firewood, etc. From the pileups at the kiln site, it is not difficult to understand how porcelains were arranged in the kiln at the time and infer the approximate number of porcelains fired each time. Unearthed specimens of celadon are jars, pots, vases, bowls, saucers, plates, dishes, cups, boxes, grinding ware and kiln furniture. Of which, bowl is the most and it accounts roughly for 90%. The most common way of decoration is incised design. Patterns incised are flora, peony, flowers, lotus-petal, lotus, wave, fish, wild goose, etc. Of which, lotus-petal and wave are most common. Based on the coloring of the glaze, the shaping, the decoration and the inscription of Chinese characters Tian Xia Tai Ping of the unearthed celadon specimens, the excavators involved believe Shantouyao kiln can be dated back to late Northern Song dynasty.

# 浙江省窑址调查

冯小琦

## 一 窑址调查概况

浙江省是故宫博物院专家学者重点进行窑址调查的省份之一。从20世纪30年代陈万里先生七去龙泉、八到浙江进行窑址调查开始，经过以后多次调查，取得了大量的第一手资料。1979年、2006年故宫博物院与浙江省考古所联合发掘了龙泉窑、德清窑遗址。2007~2010年故宫博物院的专家学者又对浙江省窑址进行了四次全面调查，到目前为止，已调查了德清的黄梅山、火烧山、亭子桥、南山、东山、苦竹坞、小马山、焦山窑，绍兴的富盛、吼山窑，上虞的小仙坛、尼姑婆、窑寺前窑， 余杭的石马斗、大陆果园窑，越窑的慈溪、寺龙口、开刀山窑， 金华的横塘、铁店窑，浦江的民生、白泥岭窑，江山的前坞、达河窑址群、碗窑村、三卿口窑，黄岩的竺家岭、凤凰山窑，永康的赵店碗金堆、瑶坛窑，武义的门牛山、小窑、新窑、蜈蚣山、瓦灶山、黄茅山、郭洞窑，衢州的沈家山、冬瓜潭、梁公塘窑，象山的黄避岙、白相头窑，龙泉的山头、大窑、金村、溪口、安仁、枫树坪官厂、杉树连山窑，东阳的葛府、歌山窑，兰溪的嵩山窑，温州的西山窑，泰顺的窑背窑，瑞安的上瓷、外三甲窑，苍南的碗窑村、龙头山、源美内、大脚岭窑，永嘉的夏壁山、启灶、钟山窑，乐清的碗窑山窑，台州的茅草山、黄家山、红沙岭、红屿埠头坦、虎头山、路桥窑，温岭的下园山、老屋山窑，临海的安王山、鲶鱼坑口、梅浦窑，遂昌的Y1、Y2窑，松阳的界首窑，云和的铁炉后、上孔青窑，庆元的竹口、潘里垄、黄坛、新窑，丽水吕步坑、保定窑，义乌的竹山里窑址群、葛塘碗窑山窑，宁海的下圆山、茶院平窑，奉化的白杜窑，临安的谢家、绍鲁窑等。

这些窑址的年代上起商周时期，下至明清时代。烧瓷品种主要有青釉、黑釉、酱褐釉、青白釉、钧釉等。

2007年至2010年进行的四次调查中，重新调查的瓷窑2007年有31处，2008年有35处，2009年有19处，2010年有1处。

其中德清、余杭、奉化、宁海、乐清、永嘉、瑞安、泰顺、苍南、义乌、临海、台州、温岭、云和、遂昌、松阳、庆元、丽水等窑是新增加的资料。

## 二 器物的主要品种

### （一）青釉瓷器

浙江是青瓷的主要产区，从北到南分布众多青瓷窑址。烧造时间从商周一直延续到明清，以宋代瓷窑数量最多。

浙江青瓷可分为四大类型——越窑型、婺州窑型、瓯窑型、龙泉窑型，以越窑型与龙泉窑型影响最大，在浙江全省分布最广。

1. 原始青瓷窑址

（1）德清窑

从商代开始烧造原始青瓷，是烧瓷时间较早的瓷窑之一。战国时期原始青瓷质量有很大提高，有的与汉代成熟瓷器相近，所以有专家认为德清窑（亭子桥窑）是中国瓷器的诞生地。

（2）绍兴窑

是原始青瓷的重要产地，与德清窑战国时期产品相类似，以青釉浅碗最为多见，碗内有明显的弦纹。采集标本有战国时期的碗、杯等，器物成型规整，胎质坚硬。

（3）萧山窑

是原始青瓷的主要产地。战国时期烧造与德清窑、绍兴窑类似的产品，弦纹浅碗最多见。

2. 早期青瓷窑址

汉代以上虞小仙坛为代表的瓷窑烧造出较为成熟的青瓷，烧造温度有些达到1310℃。魏晋南北朝时期，除上述瓷窑继续烧瓷以外，又出现一批新的瓷窑，有上虞、余杭、永嘉、台州、临海、丽水窑等。

（1）上虞窑

是早期青瓷的重要产地，从汉代到宋代延续烧造，烧瓷历史较长，瓷器质量较好。汉代小仙坛窑与新发掘的西晋尼姑婆窑所烧瓷器质量上乘，代表这一时期瓷器的较好水平。

（2）余杭窑

以往调查余杭窑主要采集有黑釉器标本，少量青釉器标本。近年的调查发现该窑烧造质量很好的青瓷，其中石马斗窑是余杭东晋时期的窑址，青釉质量较好，所烧器物有盘口壶、罐、碗等。

（3）永嘉窑

有汉、晋、唐、元、明时期窑址，早期晋代青釉瓷器有瓶、碗、洗等。

（4）台州窑

主要包括红沙岭、茅草山、虎头山、黄家山、红屿埠头坦、路桥等窑，烧制青釉、青釉褐斑器物，器类有盘口壶、鸡首壶、碗等。

（5）临海窑

采集到东晋、宋代器物标本。东晋所烧青瓷质量较好，釉色青绿、莹润光亮，工艺较精致，有些器物满釉支钉支烧，支钉细小而规整。

**3. 唐代青瓷窑址**

主要有越窑、温岭、象山、德清、丽水等窑。

（1）越窑

是唐代著名瓷窑，在前代的基础上有更大的发展。在器物的造型、釉色、装饰、工艺等方面得到进一步提高，出现一些新的器类，如注壶、三足罐、玉璧底碗、八棱瓶、长颈瓶、罂瓶、蟠龙瓶、五足炉、盒子及仿金银器造型的花式杯等。胎土细腻，施釉均匀，釉质光润，出现了历史上最好的青瓷——秘色瓷。装饰上有印花、堆塑、褐色彩绘等。支烧工艺精制，露胎部位手感平滑，没有像两晋南朝时期涩涩扎手的感觉。

（2）温岭窑

位于浙江省南部，下园山窑采集的标本质量很好。双系罐系的造型与唐代越窑双系罐一样，玉璧底碗从胎质、釉料、造型到工艺都很容易与越窑器物相混，有些碗上的划花装饰也与越窑碗十分接近。仔细观察只是釉色稍浅，有些在支烧部位稍有差别。

（3）永嘉窑

永嘉启灶窑唐代也烧造越窑风格的青瓷，器物造型、釉色、支烧工艺与越窑相同。

（4）象山、德清、丽水窑

三窑唐代烧造青瓷，胎釉质量较粗，多施半釉。器物主要有瓶、碗等。

**4. 宋代青瓷窑址**

这一时期窑址数量最多，以越窑和龙泉窑为代表，其他窑多烧造越窑、龙泉窑风格的器物，有的瓷窑既烧造越窑风格的器物，同时也烧造龙泉窑风格的器物。从地域上看，越窑周边的瓷窑多模仿越窑；偏南部龙泉窑周边的瓷窑多受龙泉窑影响。从时间方面看，同时期南北瓷窑都有烧造当时著名瓷窑风格的器物。

（1）越窑及烧制越窑风格瓷器的瓷窑

越窑。宋代越窑烧制的壶最多，并有多种形式，多以凸线把壶身分为六瓣瓜棱形，有刻花、划花装饰，肩部多有两系，系面印纹有多种。越窑上林湖窑釉色青灰，具有其特殊色调，瓷质松脆易破，应与使用瓷土原料有关。

烧制越窑风格瓷器的瓷窑主要有东阳、兰溪、鄞县、宁波、温州、临海、黄岩、宁海、奉化、浦江、衢州等。这些瓷窑烧造的瓷器在造型、釉色、装饰、烧造工艺等方面与越窑或多或少有相似之处。

东阳窑。烧瓷时间始于唐而终于北宋，遗物多青瓷，釉色变化较多，产品有精、粗两种，粗者胎质较粗，釉层薄而无光；精者胎釉细腻，釉质润泽，产品具有越窑器物风格。

兰溪窑。少数遗物具有五代越窑遗风，如浮雕莲瓣纹碗，小杯、盖盒等圈足高而外卷。宋代器物胎呈浅灰色，致使釉色青中偏淡，玻璃质强，具有独特风格。器物以注壶和碗较多，注壶的腹部为扁圆形，多饰六组双凸线，器身造型稳重之中富有秀美感。碗满釉支烧，有多种刻花装饰。此外还有瓶、罐、盒、盏托、小杯、莲瓣盘等器物。产品在烧造工艺、装饰、造型上与越窑有一定关系。

鄞县窑。郭家峙、沙叶河头与花园山窑都为五代到北宋时期瓷窑，郭家峙窑瓷质、釉色、纹饰均较窑寺前窑产品为精，标本中划花鹦鹉纹及刻花莲瓣纹器很多；造型、纹饰及支烧工艺与越窑极其近似，也属越窑体系，是继上虞窑寺前窑之后的又一重要发现。使我们得知吴越进贡中原的瓷器中一部分也仰给于此。

宁波窑。东汉至宋代瓷窑。宋代所烧器物见有执壶、瓜棱壶、罐、碗、盘、杯等，装饰与越窑的慈溪窑风格一致。

温州窑。采集标本中有与越窑划花风格近似的厚胎大碗，支烧工艺与越窑具有共同特点；各式刻花、划花碗，支烧工艺亦与越窑系瓷窑相似。釉色较越窑系青瓷为浅，保留了早期缥瓷的固有传统。

临海窑。临海梅浦窑烧造青釉、黑釉器物。主要有碗、盘、瓶、壶、钵等，青釉器物造型、釉色与越窑相似，装饰有刻划花，质量精美，与越窑相比，难分伯仲。

黄岩窑。在黄岩沙埠街一带发现了窑址群，共有窑址八处，以竺家岭窑址面积最大，所烧瓷器有精、粗之分，精者有刻鹦鹉纹者，釉色青绿，双鹦对舞，与余姚、鄞县、上虞划花鹦鹉纹风格不同；刻花菊花纹者纹饰布满整个器物，非常精美；粗者以刻花篦划纹装饰居多，纹饰线条流畅生动。

宁海窑。宁海下园山窑址青釉标本堆积不多，少量散布在匣钵等窑具之间。采集有似越窑类型的器物，烧造工艺也与越窑近似，碗等器物里心有不规则长条支痕。釉色青绿。

奉化窑。奉化白杜窑是一处五代至北宋时期的窑址。器物造型以碗为主，有少量盘、瓶、盒、壶、碟等。有些器物釉色、造型与越窑有相似之处，如凸线纹壶、碗等。在窑址采集有青釉碗，饰划花篦划纹、放射状花纹、S 形分格纹、双复线分格纹等。花式碗为外凹线。釉色深绿，与永康窑的釉色接近，双复线分格、划花篦划纹也相似。

浦江窑。宋代烧制越窑风格的凸线纹壶、大钵、碗、花式碗、外刻花瓣纹碗、盘等器物，造型、装饰与越窑相似，支烧工艺采用叠烧，有些碗心及足内留有支烧痕。不同的是浦江窑器物的釉色有些较越窑深。

衢州窑。烧制越窑风格的凸线纹执壶。釉色稍深，釉面有的较为粗糙。

（2）龙泉窑与烧制龙泉窑瓷器风格的瓷窑

龙泉窑。是浙江地区烧瓷历史较长的瓷窑。早期烧造越窑风格的器物，北宋时期及以后烧造具有自身风格的瓷器，且不同时期具有不同特点，宋、元、明初烧造质量很好的瓷器，似与宫廷用瓷有关，是一代名窑，对浙江以及江西、福建、广东等地瓷窑产生很大影响。北宋烧制青釉、青釉刻划花篦划纹瓷器，南宋烧制出粉青、梅子青釉瓷器，对后代青釉瓷器产生重要影响。

烧制龙泉窑器物风格的瓷窑主要有武义、金华、浦江、永康、衢州、江山、永嘉、丽水、遂昌、庆元、云和、松阳、乐清、苍南窑等。宋代主要仿龙泉窑划花篦划纹装饰，元明时期则仿龙泉窑青釉印花、青釉光素碗等器物。

武义窑。宋代该窑除烧造越窑风格器物以外，也烧造龙泉窑风格器物。龙泉窑风格的器物在武义郭洞、黄茅山、瓦灶山等窑址发现。宋代以烧制划花篦划纹青瓷，即所谓珠光青瓷为主。在造型、纹饰方面与龙泉窑极为相似。最具特点的碗里刻花团菊纹，内壁饰划花篦划纹或篦点纹，外壁刻线纹与龙泉窑同类器物相似。

金华窑。宋代金华横塘窑烧制划花篦划纹青瓷。有划花篦划纹碗、划花篦点花卉纹碗等。其中划花篦划纹碗中有一种内壁四等分布局，划出四个花瓣，花瓣里加篦划纹，并有分叉呈燕形，这类划花篦划纹碗有些外壁刻复线纹。

浦江窑。也烧制龙泉窑风格的划花篦划纹青瓷，有碗等。

永康窑。烧制划花篦划纹青瓷，与金华窑风格相似，多见里心划花篦划纹，外刻线纹碗；也有里心无纹饰，外刻线纹者。永康窑器物的釉色较深，是其特点。

衢州窑。烧制划花篦划纹青瓷，花纹以篦划花瓣纹较为多见，釉色青灰、青黄，部分碗心有叠烧留下的圆形支烧痕。

江山窑。江山碗窑村烧制少量划花篦划纹青瓷，器物以碗为主。

义乌窑。烧制划花篦划纹青瓷，风格与金华窑相似。

丽水窑。丽水保定窑烧制的青瓷与龙泉窑风格相似，宋代烧制划花篦划纹青瓷碗，釉色有青黄、青绿等色。

松阳窑。为唐宋时期窑址，已遭破坏，在残留约一尺多厚、2~3 米长的瓷片堆积中，主要为青釉碗、罐等瓷片，多数质量较粗。碗内有数个较大的支烧痕，多平底，有的有旋成璧足的线纹。小碗为小饼足，微内凹。釉色有青、青黄、浅青等。瓶、壶、罐多施半釉，底露胎。釉色粗黄者似金华窑青釉色泽。窑址范围内匣钵很少见，可能为裸烧，只见有喇叭形支具。有的碗造型斜直口、平底，多数似唐代造型，也有的具有宋代风格。

乐清窑。烧制的划花篦划纹碗胎色灰白，釉色有浅青、灰青，纹饰有里心刻团菊纹，内壁划花篦划纹者；有划花篦划花卉纹者；有里无装饰，外刻线纹者。采用叠烧法，有些碗心留有环形支烧痕。也有菊瓣纹折沿盘，质地稍粗。

苍南窑。也烧制少量划花篦划纹青瓷。

**5. 元明清时期青瓷窑址**

元以后这一地区主要烧造以龙泉窑为代表的龙泉窑类型的青釉瓷器，器类有碗、盘、瓶等，有些采用刻划及印花装饰。

（1）龙泉窑

龙泉窑元代青瓷窑众多，产品丰富，不仅供国内使用，还大量销往东亚、东南亚、西亚等地区。所调查的元代安仁窑，窑址瓷片堆积深厚，烧造质量很好的青瓷，釉色青翠莹润，器类有碗、盘、高足杯等。明代早期一度为宫廷烧造御用瓷器，质量上乘，在造型、纹饰方面与景德镇御窑生产的器物相似。明中期以后，龙泉窑产品在质量、数量方面都有所下降。

（2）江山窑

江山三卿口窑元代烧制龙泉窑风格的高足杯、碗、折沿盘等器物，有些碗心素胎印有阴纹折枝花卉纹。

（3）永嘉窑

永嘉钟山窑元代烧造龙泉窑风格的炉、碗、盘、高足杯等，部分器物采用叠烧，器心有环形涩胎，有的器心印有朵花纹饰。

（4）丽水窑

元代主要烧制龙泉窑风格的碗，兼少量的罐。碗胎壁较厚，有的外饰弦纹；有的采用支钉支烧，装饰有刻划花、印花，纹饰有折枝花、菊花、莲花等；有的碗里心露胎，直接垫烧。除碗以外还有少量罐。除青釉以外还有黑褐釉小碗，也采用支钉支烧。窑具有研磨器、垫圈、垫饼等。

（5）庆元窑

庆元新窑西距市区 20 里，窑址在竹口镇新窑村，瓯江从乡间流过。烧造龙泉窑系产品，器类有碗、折沿花口盘。有简单的刻划花装饰。碗足小，底心有釉，垫饼支烧。竹口窑是元明时期窑址，窑址在竹口镇路边的山上，分布在长约 2 公里范围内。上山可以见到窑具与瓷片，窑具较多，瓷片混杂其间。碗有带“福”字、“清”字和阴文印花的，带字者，外壁多刻线纹，与福建闽清窑器物类似，另有盘、罐、盖、炉、灯、卧足杯等多种，特别是炉的造型非常丰富，有筒式三足炉、扁腹三足炉、饼足三足炉、乳丁刻花三兽足炉及八卦纹炉等。

（6）云和窑

元明时期烧造龙泉窑类型的青釉瓷器，元代器类有碗、高足碗、折沿盘等，装饰有阴纹印花，纹饰有莲花等折枝花卉。有些碗外壁刻莲瓣纹装饰。

明代有些碗外口沿划刻线纹装饰。

（7）遂昌窑

元代常见厚胎碗，外刻突起的莲瓣纹。有的里心刻朵花纹，有的好像有“清”字。从釉色看有似龙泉窑风格的，也有似越窑风格的。器物足部修坯较规矩，足底心垫饼支烧。器类有碗、盘等，盘有折沿的。质量总体比较好。有的釉色很漂亮，似粉青；有的釉色深绿青翠；有的釉色泛黄。胎釉致密。有的器物甚至与龙泉好者不相上下。窑具有匣钵、垫饼、支具等。

明代器物胎釉较元代的粗很多，工艺也粗糙。多采用器心无釉直接垫烧。里心素胎者印有图案花纹或文字，图案花纹有马、折枝花卉、折枝梅花、银锭、小鸟、双鱼；文字有“广”、“常”、“福”、“寿”、“和”、“利”、“清”、“满”、“象”、“春”等。釉色有青黄、青绿。器类有碗、折沿盘等。匣钵有M形，垫饼有圆形、圆饼带小托形。

**（二）青白釉瓷器**

青白釉瓷器在浙江的西南及南部发现，在江山达河、衢州冬瓜潭、苍南碗窑村窑烧造。

（1）江山窑

烧造青釉、黑釉、青白釉瓷器。因距江西较近，青白瓷与景德镇窑相似，釉色青白。多小件器物，以炉、瓶、罐、壶、盒、高足杯等为常见，装饰多见细线阳文印花，其中八卦纹三足炉数量较多，与景德镇窑同类器形相似。阳文印花瓶、壶、罐等与福建德化、浦城窑的器物风格相似。

（2）衢州窑

以烧制青釉、青釉褐彩、酱黑釉器物为主，在衢州冬瓜潭窑址发现少量青白釉器物，以碗为主，釉色青白，器形较小，与其青釉、青釉褐彩多大件器物明显不同。

（3）苍南窑

位于浙江省南部，距福建较近，主要烧造青釉、黑釉和青白釉。在苍南碗窑村发现烧造青白釉瓷器的窑址，主要烧造缸、碗类器皿，装饰有划花篦划纹、外刻线纹。器物从釉色、造型、装饰看与福建地区青白瓷相似。

**（三）黑釉瓷器**

浙江地区以烧青瓷为主，兼烧黑瓷。目前发现烧造黑瓷的窑有德清、余杭、武义、温岭、江山、衢州、金华、临安、泰顺、庆元、丽水等。

1. 早期黑釉瓷窑

（1）德清窑和余杭窑

两窑是浙江地区烧造黑瓷较早的瓷窑，同时也烧造青瓷。东晋时期烧造质量很好的黑瓷，器类有鸡首壶、盘口壶、唾壶、碗、灯、砚等。其中在德清窑的原始瓷中就已经出现了黑瓷，以后持续烧造直到唐代，是烧造黑瓷时间较长的瓷窑。

（2）温岭窑

在温岭下园山窑址发现有唐代花瓷拍鼓，造型及花斑很像河南鲁山窑的产品。胎质坚硬，很细润，其产地有待于进一步研究。此外有黑釉壶等标本。

2. 宋代黑釉瓷窑

（1）温岭窑

温岭窑唐宋时期烧制越窑风格青瓷，在老屋山与下园山两处窑址发现黑瓷标本。在老屋山窑址采集有宋代黑釉瓶、罐、碗等器物，釉色为酱黑，质地较粗。碗采用直接叠烧，碗心留有叠烧留下的痕迹。

（2）武义窑

烧造品种较多，主要有龙泉窑风格的青瓷，包括珠光青瓷，此外还烧造黑釉、钧釉器物。在武义的蜈蚣山、郭洞等窑发现黑釉器物标本，以碗为主，釉色较黑，施釉不到足，有的釉色出现蓝色窑变。碗口有折度，小圈足，造型为典型的茶盏样式。

（3）江山窑

江山窑烧制青白釉、青釉、黑釉器物，在江山达河窑址群采集到黑釉标本，器物造型有双系罐、灯、碗、盘等。双系罐釉色为酱黑色，碗有几种造型，有茶盏式、浅式，有的口部有折痕，有的口部装饰青釉。有些碗、盘采用刮圈叠烧，碗心留有圆形涩胎。

（4）衢州窑

衢州冬瓜潭、梁公塘、沈家山窑都烧制黑釉器物，主要有瓶、壶、罐、碗、杯、碟等。釉色为酱黑色。碗有花式。碗、碟采用叠烧，有些器心有支钉痕。

（5）金华窑

金华铁店窑烧制青釉、黑釉器物，黑釉器物有瓶、罐。金华横塘窑烧制黑釉瓶、碗等，釉色为酱黑色。

（6）临安窑

在临安的绍鲁、谢家两处窑址采集到黑釉标本，黑釉碗有些胎质较白而坚硬，口部有折痕，有的口部饰青釉；敞口浅碗一般足部修坯不甚规整。标本中有黑釉、青白釉叠烧在一起的，可以看出两个品种是同窑烧制的。还有些酱黑釉瓶、罐类器物。

（7）泰顺窑

烧造越窑、龙泉窑风格的青瓷，也烧制少量黑釉瓷器，质量较粗，釉色非纯黑，而是酱黑色釉。采用支钉支烧，碗心留有六个较大的支烧痕。

（8）庆元窑

庆元窑主要烧造龙泉窑风格的青釉瓷器，庆元潘里垄窑宋代烧造黑釉瓷器。器物以小盏为主，造型小巧，胎色较深，釉色有酱黑釉、黑釉，有的釉漆黑光亮，质量较好。在造型、釉色、胎色上都与建阳窑有相似之处。碗有折口与敞口各式。

**（四）钧釉瓷器**

浙江地区的钧釉瓷器主要产自金华、衢州地区，金华铁店、武义郭洞、义乌竹山里、越窑开刀山等窑烧造。

（1）金华铁店窑

铜釉器物造型较为丰富，见有大碗、小盏、罐、瓶、炉、鼓钉洗、高足碗、花盆等。少量碗上有刻花装饰。碗采用直接叠烧与支钉垫烧，碗心留有支烧痕。胎色较深，釉色有蓝、灰蓝等色，也有在灰蓝地上饰深褐色釉，似花釉的。其产品外销到东南亚，韩国新安海底沉船上打捞有该窑的花盆、鼓钉洗、高足碗等。

（2）武义郭洞窑

烧瓷品种有青釉、黑釉、钧釉。采集的标本有钧釉大碗及小盏，釉色与金华铁店窑相似，胎色较深，釉色以蓝白色窑变为主，烧法亦采用叠烧。

（3）义乌竹山里窑

主要烧造钧釉大小碗、盏、折沿盘等器物，釉色与金华铁店窑相似。烧造方法采用叠烧，外施釉至近足部。

（4）越窑开刀山窑

在早期越窑青釉中，会出现窑变现象，这在浙江地区青瓷中较为常见。有些是在青釉器物局部出现蓝色窑变，有些则通体出现蓝色窑变。如晋时的耳杯、鸟形杯等。南宋时期烧造乳浊釉青瓷，器物有瓶、碗等。

## 三　器物的造型、装饰及工艺特点

**（一）造型**

浙江地区瓷器总体上造型规整，多数胎质较为细腻。以越窑、龙泉窑、官窑为代表的瓷器质量上乘。

1. 战国时期

虽然此时处于瓷器初创阶段，但由于瓷器受铜器造型的影响，在器物成型方面特点突出。器物线条刚硬，棱角分明，与铜器造型线条相似。

2. 汉代

浙江地区成功烧成青釉瓷器，有壶、罐、博山炉等器物。

3. 魏晋南北朝时期

此时是浙江青瓷大发展的阶段，窑口众多，器类丰富，有壶、盘口壶、鸡首壶、罐、渣斗、折沿洗、虎子、格盘、碗、盘、砚、盘口瓶、灯、熏等，可以看出瓷器已经逐渐取代铜器、漆器、陶器，成为当时人们生活中不可或缺的器物，陈设、日常用具应有尽有。在造型上善于用动物形象装饰器物，如鸡首壶、熊形灯、鹰形尊、神兽形尊、蛙式水盂、羊形器、辟邪等。

4. 唐代

国力强盛，文化发达，青瓷得到更大地发展，越窑青瓷的质量更加精美，秘色瓷是其中的最好代表。器物造型更加丰富，有八棱瓶、长颈瓶、罂瓶、注壶、倒流壶、罐、三足罐、盒、枕、杯、灯、水盂等，不论壶、罐还是碗、盘都喜用花瓣来装饰，且多为四瓣，如四瓣瓜棱壶、罐，四出口碗、盘等，形成唐代特有的造型风格。唐代越窑双系罐也是很有特色的，系呈椭圆形，上有圆孔，下有椭圆形装饰，构成了越窑类型青瓷常见系的形式。

5. 宋代

是中国瓷器发展历史上瓷窑众多的阶段，瓷器制造业空前发展，各窑烧制具有自身特点的器物。器物造型种类比以往任何时候都丰富，有执壶、罐、瓶、供器、花盆、渣斗、炉、盒、碗、盏托、盘、碟、盆、熏炉、枕等，每一种器物又有多种样式。宋代也用花瓣来装饰器物，一般多为六瓣，如六瓣瓜棱壶、瓜棱罐，六出口碗、盘，构成了宋代瓷器的造型特点。多瓣形此时也开始流行，如菊瓣纹，装饰在壶、盒、碗、盘上。壶以越窑青釉壶为代表，壶系很有特点，双系圆孔，上呈三角形或圆形，下呈长方形，上面印有各种纹饰，纹饰多达几十种，其功用不仅仅是穿绳系带，而且作为装饰。此为越窑首创，影响一批瓷窑纷纷模仿。

6. 元代

浙江地区瓷器以龙泉窑烧瓷为代表，胎体较为厚重，大件器物有的高达 70 厘米以上，小件器物只有几厘米。产品不仅供国内使用，也远销到国外。常见大瓶、罐、花盆、高足碗、盘、鼓钉洗、洗等。在造型方面的突出特点是烧制连座器物，如连座瓶、连座罐等。

（二）装饰

1. 胎装饰

浙江历代青釉瓷器采用划花、镂空、贴塑、浮雕、印花、刻花、戳印等装饰，有些时代风格明显。

（1）划花装饰

划花水波纹装饰多见于汉代瓷器，一般是在器物如盘口壶、罐等的肩部划数道水波纹；划花莲瓣纹装饰常见于南朝时期，也是时代风格明显的装饰之一，饰于瓶、罐、壶、碗外或盘内，多二三道细线划出，有的在盘上莲瓣纹中心还饰莲蓬纹。

唐代越窑开始流行划花装饰，一般为粗线条划花，多在碗、杯里心划刻简单的花卉纹。五代到宋代流行细线划花，花纹种类丰富，有花卉纹、花鸟纹、人物纹等。

划花篦划（点）纹以龙泉窑为代表的一批瓷窑广泛采用，流行于北宋晚期到南宋时期，常饰于碗、盘内。纹饰刻划并用，间用篦梳样工具划出篦划纹或者篦点纹，有些在碗外还刻成组的线纹，即所谓的“珠光青瓷”，成为宋代南方瓷窑青瓷、青白瓷中最常用的装饰之一。

（2）镂空装饰

是浙江地区历代瓷窑常采用的装饰。在战国时期的瓷器上就已使用镂空装饰，以后作为常用装饰用于瓶、熏炉、熏篮、博山炉、套盒、器盖、枕等上，镂空形式有三角形、叶形、卷枝形、花形等。

（3）贴塑铺首装饰

汉代到西晋时期比较常见，是仿铜器造型而来，对称装饰，有的与带状印纹一起使用。

（4）浮雕装饰

五代到宋代越窑流行浮雕或刻莲瓣纹装饰，五代到宋初莲瓣宽大肥厚，影响北方定窑、耀州窑等窑。

（5）印花装饰

一种是带状印纹装饰，时代特征明显，多见于西晋时期，常饰于器物的肩、腹部。一般是带状网格纹，有的在网格纹上下饰有联珠纹。到东晋时期，网格纹基本消失，只见联珠纹。另一种为印花花卉纹，唐代越窑器物中有的采用阳文印花，常见于杯里心，花纹凸起而简单。龙泉窑元代瓷器大量采用印花装饰，有阴纹、阳纹之分，也有露胎与施釉之别，如双鱼纹、人物纹、花果纹等。

刻印莲瓣纹是以龙泉窑为代表的一批瓷窑多采用的装饰方式，南宋到元代比较流行。

用文字来装饰器物的有元代龙泉窑，大罐上面印“清香美酒”四字。

（6）刻花装饰

流行于越窑、龙泉窑类型的瓷窑。在器物上刻出花瓣、莲瓣纹，刻花线条较粗，有浮雕感。

（7）戳印纹装饰

在越窑类型瓷器上使用，常见碗、盘等器物外口沿划莲瓣纹，中心戳印莲蓬、莲子纹。

**2. 釉彩装饰**

（1）褐彩装饰

东晋时期流行点彩装饰，在器物的口沿、肩部、腹部以及鸡首壶鸡首的眼睛等部位施以褐色点彩。越窑、台州窑、临海窑都烧青釉点彩器物，唐宋时期除点彩外，流行褐色彩绘，以越窑、临海窑、衢州窑为代表。

越窑。除使用点彩外，唐代出现褐色彩绘，在青釉罂、炉上以褐色彩绘云纹，风格独特。

台州窑。东晋时期烧造青釉瓷器，釉色稍浅，装饰褐色斑点也较为普遍。已发现台州红屿埠头坦、虎头山、黄家山、茅草山、红沙岭窑址烧制褐色点彩器物，在壶、罐、碗、洗的口沿饰褐色点彩。

临海安王山、鲶鱼坑口窑。都烧制青釉褐色点彩器物，在盘口壶、罐、碗等器物的口沿点褐彩，有二点一组、三点一组等排列方法。

温州窑。在青釉器上用褐彩绘树叶纹，也较特别。

衢州冬瓜潭、梁公塘窑。烧青釉、黑釉、褐釉、青白釉品种，青釉中有加褐彩者，器物有执壶、罐、器盖、缸、盆等，所绘纹饰有花卉纹、鱼纹等，花纹较为简练。

### （三）工艺特点

浙江地区的支烧窑具有匣钵、垫饼、支圈、齿状垫具、圆饼形支钉等。原始瓷采用叠烧，支具为圆形带窝，3~5 个垫珠不等；魏晋南北朝时期多采用碗状齿形支具与圆饼上几个大支钉支具，器物上留有数个较大的支痕；唐代器物也采用支钉支烧，支烧痕多在足上；五代至宋一般采用垫圈支烧，龙泉窑采用垫饼支烧，官窑的支具为圆饼上出一个至多个支钉。

## 四　小结

浙江地区烧瓷时间早，延续历史长，瓷窑数量多，越窑、郊坛官窑、龙泉窑等为该地区著名瓷窑，对很多瓷窑产生很大影响。烧瓷品种以青釉为主，还有青白釉、黑釉、钧釉等品种。装饰有胎装饰与釉彩装饰，胎装饰以划花、印花、刻花为主，兼有镂空、堆塑、戳印、浮雕等技法；釉彩装饰主要为褐色斑点与褐色彩绘，还有用两种不同色釉装饰一件器物的。不同时期有不同品种，如西晋带状印纹、东晋褐斑、南北朝莲瓣纹、唐代印花、宋代划花篦划纹，都具有时代特征。烧造主要采用支烧和垫烧，在器物上留下特有的痕迹。

浙江地区瓷窑唐代到元代产品不仅供国内使用，还销往国外，主要有越窑、龙泉窑、金华窑。

# The Investigation of Kiln Sites Located in Zhejiang Province

Feng Xiaoqi

Zhejiang Province is an important source of ancient Chinese porcelains. A great number of kiln sites of different time periods have been found throughout the province. There are many famous kilns in the province. The best known are Yue kiln, Longquan kiln, Wuzhou kiln, kilns in Wenzhou area and so on. Kilns in the province had never stopped producing porcelains ever since Shang dynasty when primitive celadon was first produced. Porcelains made by the kilns in the old time are predominately green glaze with diverse decorations. Porcelains from Shang dynasty to Han dynasty are usually with incised or stamped design; while in Three Kingdoms and Western Jin dynasty, porcelains with stamped design in stripes and coated molds were prevailing; those of Eastern Jin dynasty are normally with brown color decoration; during Southern Dynasties, porcelains with incised design of lotus petals were popular; those of Tang dynasty were frequently seen with stamped design; from Five Dynasties to Song dynasty, porcelains are usually with fine-incised design or comb-incised patterns, comb-incised dots and brown color decoration; those of Yuan and Ming dynasty are commonly with stamped design which is unique in style. Some kilns of Eastern Jin dynasty, Tang and Song dynasty also produced black glaze porcelains. And some kilns of Song and Yuan dynasty produced bluish white glaze and Jun glaze wares as well.

# 窑址调查纪要

| 窑址 | 调查时间 | 调查人 |
|---|---|---|
| 德清窑 | 1981.12 | 冯先铭　李毅华 |
| | 2006.5 | 冯小琦　蔡　毅　董健丽　黄卫文 |
| | 2007.12 | 冯小琦　董健丽　赵　山　王桂林 |
| 余杭窑 | 1979.7 | 冯先铭　李辉柄　王莉英　叶佩兰　欧志培 |
| | 2007.12 | 冯小琦　董健丽　赵　山　王桂林 |
| 郊坛官窑 | 1954.7 | 陈万里　冯先铭 |
| | 2007.11 | 冯小琦　董健丽　赵　山　李友来 |
| 萧山窑 | 1981.12 | 冯先铭　李毅华 |
| | 2006.5 | 冯小琦　黄卫文 |
| 临安窑 | 2010.10 | 冯小琦　赵聪月　高晓然　刘志岗　王桂林 |
| 绍兴窑 | 1981.12 | 冯先铭　李毅华 |
| | 2007.12 | 冯小琦　董健丽　赵　山　王桂林 |
| 上虞窑 | 1978.6 | 叶喆民 |
| | 1979.7 | 冯先铭　李辉柄　王莉英　叶佩兰 |
| | 2007.12 | 冯小琦　董健丽　赵　山　王桂林 |
| 越　窑 | 1954.11 | 陈万里　冯先铭 |
| | 1979.7 | 冯先铭　李辉柄　王莉英　叶佩兰　欧志培 |
| | 1981.12 | 冯先铭　李毅华 |
| | 2008.1 | 冯小琦　董健丽　赵　山　李友来 |
| 宁波窑 | 1979.7 | 冯先铭　李辉柄　王莉英　叶佩兰　欧志培 |
| | 2009.12 | 冯小琦　董健丽　刘志岗　李友来 |
| 鄞县窑 | 1981.12 | 冯先铭　李毅华 |
| | 2009.12 | 冯小琦　董健丽　刘志岗　李友来 |
| 奉化窑 | 2009.12 | 冯小琦　董健丽　刘志岗　李友来 |
| 象山窑 | 1974.10 | 李知宴 |
| | 1981.12 | 冯先铭　李毅华 |
| | 2009.12 | 冯小琦　董健丽　刘志岗　李友来 |

| | | | | | |
|---|---|---|---|---|---|
| 宁海窑 | 2009.12 | 冯小琦 | 董健丽 | 刘志岗 | 李友来 |
| 临海窑 | 2008.1 | 冯小琦 | 董健丽 | 赵　山 | 李友来 |
| 黄岩窑 | 1979.7 | 冯先铭 | 李辉柄 | 王莉英 | 叶佩兰 |
| | | 欧志培 | | | |
| | 2008.1 | 冯小琦 | 董健丽 | 赵　山 | 李友来 |
| 台州窑 | 2008.1 | 冯小琦 | 董健丽 | 赵　山 | 李友来 |
| 温岭窑 | 2008.1 | 冯小琦 | 董健丽 | 赵　山 | 李友来 |
| 乐清窑 | 2008.1 | 冯小琦 | 董健丽 | 赵　山 | 李友来 |
| 永嘉窑 | 1954.11 | 陈万里 | 冯先铭 | | |
| | 2007.12 | 冯小琦 | 董健丽 | 赵　山 | 王桂林 |
| 温州窑 | 1954.11 | 陈万里 | 冯先铭 | | |
| | 1979.7 | 冯先铭 | 李辉柄 | 王莉英 | 叶佩兰 |
| | | 欧志培 | | | |
| 瑞安窑 | 2007.12 | 冯小琦 | 董健丽 | 赵　山 | 王桂林 |
| 苍南窑 | 2007.12 | 冯小琦 | 董健丽 | 赵　山 | 王桂林 |
| 泰顺窑 | 2007.12 | 冯小琦 | 董健丽 | 赵　山 | 王桂林 |
| 兰溪窑 | 1981.12 | 冯先铭 | 李毅华 | | |
| | 1983.11 | 冯先铭 | 李毅华 | | |
| | 2009.12 | 冯小琦 | 董健丽 | 刘志岗 | 李友来 |
| 浦江窑 | 1983.11 | 冯先铭 | 李毅华 | | |
| | 2009.12 | 冯小琦 | 董健丽 | 刘志岗 | 李友来 |
| 金华窑 | 1981.12 | 冯先铭 | 李毅华 | 李辉柄 | 冯小琦 |
| | 2008.1 | 冯小琦 | 董健丽 | 赵　山 | 李友来 |
| 武义窑 | 1978.7 | 冯先铭 | 李辉柄 | 李知宴 | |
| | 1979.6 | 冯先铭 | 李辉柄 | 王莉英 | 叶佩兰 |
| | | 欧志培 | | | |
| | 2004.10 | 李辉柄 | 冯小琦 | | |
| | 2008.1 | 冯小琦 | 董健丽 | 赵　山 | 李友来 |
| 义乌窑 | 2009.12 | 冯小琦 | 董健丽 | 刘志岗 | 李友来 |

| | | |
|---|---|---|
| 永康窑 | 1983.11 | 冯先铭　李毅华 |
| | 2009.12 | 冯小琦　董健丽　赵　山　李友来 |
| 东阳窑 | 1981.12 | 冯先铭　李毅华 |
| | 2009.12 | 冯小琦　董健丽　刘志岗　李友来 |
| 龙游窑 | 1983.11 | 冯先铭　李毅华 |
| | 2008.1 | 冯小琦　董健丽　赵　山　李友来 |
| 衢州窑 | 1983.11 | 冯先铭　李毅华 |
| | 2008.1 | 冯小琦　董健丽　赵　山　李友来 |
| 江山窑 | 1981.12 | 冯先铭　李毅华 |
| | 2008.1 | 冯小琦　董健丽　赵　山　李友来 |
| 遂昌窑 | 2009.12 | 冯小琦　董健丽　刘志岗　李友来 |
| 松阳窑 | 2009.12 | 冯小琦　董健丽　刘志岗　李友来 |
| 丽水窑 | 2007.12 | 冯小琦　董健丽　赵　山　王桂林 |
| 云和窑 | 2009.12 | 冯小琦　董健丽　刘志岗　李友来 |
| 龙泉窑 | 1954.11 | 陈万里　冯先铭 |
| | 1979.6 | 冯先铭　李辉柄　王莉英　叶佩兰　欧志培 |
| | 1979 | 李知宴　何俊义 |
| | 1981.12 | 冯先铭　李毅华 |
| | 2004.10 | 李辉柄　冯小琦 |
| | 2007.11 | 冯小琦　董健丽　赵　山　王桂林 |
| 庆元窑 | 2009.12 | 冯小琦　董健丽　刘志岗　李友来 |

注：以上统计以故宫博物院现存瓷片为准，无标本的调查不计在内。

# 后记

《故宫博物院藏中国古代窑址标本》一套书经过近20年的酝酿，今天终于要逐卷面世了。本书是由故宫博物院几代陶瓷研究者——陈万里、冯先铭、李辉柄、叶喆民、王莉英、叶佩兰、李知宴、何俊义、欧志培、刘兰华、李毅华、邵长波、杨静荣、冯小琦、蔡毅、吕成龙、徐巍、王健华、刘伟、纪伟、董健丽、赵聪月、郑宏、高晓然、郭玉昆、韩倩、黄卫文、赵晓春等深入考古第一线采集的众多标本汇集而成。这些标本的收集历经了半个多世纪，经过三次大的整理。第一次是在1988年，由冯先铭先生负责，参加者有刘兰华、冯小琦、纪伟，主要整理存放在故宫文华殿与研究室的标本；第二次是在2004年，由冯小琦负责，主要参加者有杨静荣、蔡毅、刘伟，是在第一次的基础上，把数十年散放在承乾宫、永寿宫等数处的标本集中整理。整理工作从搬运开始，逐个开箱、清洗，并分省按窑口进行编目；第三次从2008年至今，由冯小琦负责，董健丽、韩倩参加。在前两次的基础上，对所有标本进行重新排柜位，核对数字，特别是对2005年以后调查的标本进行整理、拍照，对前两次整理的遗留问题进行解决。窑址标本文字介绍以冯先铭先生关于古窑址的论述为基础，由冯小琦进行整理与补充。附图说明由董健丽、韩倩完成。此书得以出版，特别要感谢各级领导的大力支持与协调，感谢陶瓷组全体同人的合作，感谢资料信息中心的全力支持与配合。感谢各地博物馆、考古部门以及各地文保单位对故宫窑址调查工作的大力支持。

冯小琦

2014年10月

图书在版编目（CIP）数据

故宫博物院藏中国古代窑址标本．浙江 / 故宫博物院编．
-- 北京 ：故宫出版社，2015.7
ISBN 978-7-5134-0731-1

Ⅰ．①故… Ⅱ．①故… Ⅲ．①古代陶瓷-标本-中国-图录②古代陶瓷-标本-浙江省-图录 Ⅳ．① K876.32

中国版本图书馆 CIP 数据核字 (2015) 第 057172 号

**故宫博物院藏中国古代窑址标本**

**浙江**

编　　者：故宫博物院
出版发行：故宫出版社
地址：北京东城区景山前街4号　邮编：100009
电话：010-85007808　010-85007816　传真：010-65129479
网址：www.culturefc.cn
邮箱：ggcb@culturefc.cn
制版印刷：北京雅昌艺术印刷有限公司
开　　本：878×1092毫米　1/16
印　　张：91.75
版　　次：2015年7月第1版
2015年7月第1次印刷
书　　号：ISBN 978-7-5134-0731-1
定　　价：660.00元（全三册）